The Devil Knows

David J Cooper

Published by David J Cooper, 2017.

THE DEVIL KNOWS

First edition. March 15, 2017.

Written by David J Cooper.

Table of Contents

For Angela Birds, my number one fan.

Introduction

It was the swinging sixties. Manchester and Liverpool were rivals in the football league and the Mersey beat sound was dominating the charts with Freddie and the Dreamers at the top of the hit parade. But high on the moors above the city Ian Brady and Myra Hindley were forging their places in history as a new breed of serial killer.

Their depravity shocked and sickened the nation and left five families destitute. They escaped the death penalty by a matter of months which left the British taxpayer paying for their upkeep in jail.

But what made them turn into sadistic killers?

They admitted to five murders but how many did they really commit?

How many more missing children are still buried on the moors?

How could they take innocent lives without turning a hair?

This story is about their relationship and the plans they made to satisfy their lust.

Maybe you will find the answers here.

CAUTION!!!!

The book contains very strong language and graphic sexual content. It also contains parts which some readers might find disturbing.

CHAPTER ONE

She sat at her desk glancing across the office at the tall, mysterious, good looking clerk who was too busy to notice her. Her left hand tugged at her tight black skirt. The cool breeze from the fan lifted her bleached blonde hair and ruffled her white, figure hugging blouse. It was important for her to look good on her first day at Millwards Merchandising but she didn't want to appear as if she was trying too hard and definitely didn't want others to think she was a tart.

Something about the clerk had ignited a flame within her. She had fallen in love with a complete stranger and was determined that he should fall for her as well.

She never believed in love at first sight but it had happened to her. But she was going to find out later that his beauty was only skin deep.

"Good morning," she said.

He didn't look up. Not taking the slightest interest in her he waved his fingers acknowledging her and continued with his work.

Taken aback by his coldness she stopped tugging at her skirt and slumped back in her chair.

She didn't want to stare but her eyes kept flicking to him.

"How could he ignore me?" she thought to herself. "Just my luck. He's probably queer. Well I'm not giving in that easily. I'll make sure he takes interest in me one way or another."

The door opened and in walked Tom Craig the head of the company.

His appearance was nothing special. His twinkling eyes were framed by thick rimmed spectacles and there were grey whiskers on his stubble chin.

"Good morning Ian," he said nodding to the mysterious clerk. "Do you know where Bert is?" "He's just gone to the bog," Brady replied.

"Well while I'm waiting for him," said Tom. "Let me introduce you to Miss Hindley our new typist."

"This is Myra Hindley," he said introducing her to Brady."And this is Ian Brady."

"Nice to meet you, Ian," she said reaching her hand out.

"Mr Brady to you," he snapped in a strong Scottish

accent. "My name's Mr Brady."

"Come on Ian," Tom said. "Go easy on the lass. It's her first day here."

Turning to Myra he said, "Take no notice of him. He probably got out of the wrong side of the bed this morning."

"I see," she said looking a bit taken aback by Brady's rudeness.

"Don't fret lass," he said. Turning to Brady he asked,

"Did you say that Bert had gone to the lavatory?"

"That's what he said," replied Brady shuffling through the paperwork on his desk.

"When he comes back will you tell him to come to my office?"

"Okay," he replied. "Will do."

Myra glanced over at Brady cursing under her breath that he hadn't even bothered to shake hands with her when she had been formally introduced.

"What kind of man is he?" she thought. "He looks as if he's a selfish, hard hearted bastard. He's crude but very sexy. And I love a man with greased hair."

She was deep in thought about Brady when a tap on the shoulder made her jump.

"Could you take some dictation, Miss Hindley?" asked Bert Matthews.

Bert was the head clerk and was going to retire at Christmas. He had been working for some years at Millwards and knew that Ian Brady was ready to step into his shoes.

His face was slightly wrinkled and the lines around his eyes told of laughter and affection. His worries of the past and of the present showed in the lines on his forehead.

"Oh you startled me," she said. "Yes of course. When you are ready."

"I think you need to go to see Tom Craig first," Brady called over to him. "He's been here looking for you but you were in the shit house."

"I was in the lavatory if you don't mind," Bert said.

Nodding towards Myra, "Why do you have to be so vulgar and especially in front of a young woman?" he asked.

"I'm sure she's heard stronger language." he replied. "She doesn't look that innocent to me."

She got out of her chair and was about to go for him when Bert said, "Ignore him lass. He's trying to wind you up. Don't fall for it. Don't come down to his level."

Biting her lips she sat back down and continued working.

But Brady's attitude was drawing her further towards him.

"It's like chain smoking," she thought. "One after the other. An addiction and that's how this bloke is affecting me."

Her first day in her new job had been different and she couldn't wait to get home and tell her sister Maureen about the new love in her life.

"Mo," she said grabbing her sister by the hand. "There's this bloke in the office and I've fallen head over heels for him."

"Don't be barmy," replied Maureen. "How can you fall for someone when you don't even know them?"

"I can't explain," she replied. "But I know this is the real thing. He's so slick and handsome and much more interesting than Ronnie, my ex. I always had the dream of falling in love with somebody like James Dean or Elvis Presley. Ian is both of them rolled into one."

"Oh our Myra. How can you talk such shit?" Maureen asked.

"He's very mysterious," she replied. "He is very vulgar and I find this sexy in him and he turns me on."

Fumbling in her bag she continued. "Do you know I got so excited thinking about him that my knickers got damp."

Pulling a pair of pink briefs from her bag, "I had to go to the lavvy and take them off. Look!" she said waving them in her hand.

"You're disgusting our Myra," said Maureen. "Put them away before gran comes in."

Maureen was slim and attractive. She was four years younger than Myra. She

had her dark brown hair shaped in the beehive style. It suited her perfectly sculpted face.

Myra had lived at her gran's house just after Maureen had been born. She loved her gran a lot because she could do anything she wanted.

Her gran idolized her. She always knew more than she let on, but unlike Myra's mother she never said "I told you so." She was her angel and hero. Her crumpled face was part of who she was.

"Ian, eh," Maureen tutted. "And what does Ian think of all of this?"

"I've no idea," she replied shrugging her shoulders. "He doesn't speak to me. He just throws insults."

"And that's love at first sight?" Maureen asked.

"It is for me," she replied. "But don't worry. I'm working on it and you will see that Ian will be at my feet before long."

Shaking her head, "what a load of bollocks," Maureen said.

The days turned into weeks. The weeks into months and Myra was getting nowhere with Ian until she noticed one day that he was reading a book profoundly.

"Excuse me Mr. Matthews," she asked Bert. "What's the title of that book Mr Brady is reading?"

"It's called Mein Kampf," he replied.

"Is it German?" she asked.

"To be quite honest lass I'm not sure," he replied. "I think it's written in English but I do know that he studies German."

Slowly raising her eyebrows, "Interesting," she sighed.

"You fancy him don't you?" Bert asked.

"What makes you say that?" she asked biting her lip.

"I'm not a mind reader, chuck," he replied. "It's written all over your face. Just bide your time. Get him to notice you. Play hard to get and I think that will get him interested. He'll like that."

"Are you sure?" she asked.

"I've known him ever since he started working here," he replied. "He's dedicated to his work. He likes to have a bet on the horses but gets very pissed off when his horse loses. He has a vile temper when he's pissed off.

She left her desk and went over to where Bert was sitting out of earshot of Brady.

"I do like him a lot," she said. "He's very good looking and interesting. Do you know if he has a girlfriend?"

"I don't think he does," he replied. "I can't be sure. He's never talked about having one. I tell you what I'll do. I'll get him to have a game of chess with me in the lunch break tomorrow. While we're playing you can sit somewhere nearby and get him to notice you. I'll mention you to him during the game."

"That's very good of you," she said and went back to her desk.

After work she went straight to the library and borrowed poetry books by Wordsworth and Longfellow.

"If Ian can see I'm interested in books maybe he'll show interest in me," she thought to herself.

It was the lunch break and Myra was going to make sure Ian noticed her that day. He had been ignoring her as was the norm but today was going to be the make or break.

She went outside with her sandwiches and saw him playing chess with Bert.

She casually walked past them and deliberately let her skirt brush against the side of Brady's head.

Glancing up at her, "Do you mind?" he asked.

"Not if you don't," she replied.

"Cocky little twat," he said, his eyes mocking her.

"Come on Ian," Bert said. "She's a pretty little thing. I think she fancies you. Why don't you go and chat to her?"

She sat on the lawn nearby and started to flick through the pages of her books of poetry.

Brady had noticed that she had got some books under her arm when her skirt brushing against his head had interrupted his game of chess. He was curious to know what they were about.

He got up and walked over to her.

"I see that you read books as well Miss Hindley," he said.

"I'm sorry," she said as if she hadn't heard him.

Raising his voice slightly he repeated, "I see that you read books as well."

"Yes, I find reading very interesting," she said lying through her teeth.

"Do you mind if I take a look?" he asked.

"Be my guest," she replied.

Looking over her shoulder and rubbing his nose he asked, "Wordsworth. So you like reading Wordsworth?"

A hot flush raced through her body. It felt as though she was standing next to a furnace. Her eyes met his and she replied, "I love all kinds of poetry but Wordsworth is my favourite. My favourite poem is I wandered lonely as a cloud."

"So you like Hiawatha as well," he asked trying to impress her.

"Hiawatha was written by Longfellow," she replied. "Look. I have his poetry here too."

His face turned red as he looked down and said, "I like reading but I'm not into poetry. I'm surprised to see you reading, especially poetry. I thought you were just like the other young birds who just like to go out and get pissed at the weekend."

"I don't go out much," she replied. "I live with my gran. I understand you like reading as well."

"How do you know?" he asked.

Smiling at him she said, "A little bird told me."

"I'm reading Mein Kampf. Hitler wrote it," he replied. "I'm fascinated with him and the Nazis."

"Is it written in German?" she asked. "I can't speak German."

"Of course," he replied. "Hitler was German. I've been studying German for quite a while now and I understand what the book's about. It's a fascinating read."

"I see," she said.

"You said you lived with your gran, didn't you?" he asked.

"That's right," she replied.

"Don't you go out?" he asked.

"No," she replied. "I used to go out with my sister, Maureen, but she's got a boyfriend now."

"Don't you have a boyfriend?" he asked.

"I did," she replied. "But he was boring so I packed him in. I'm looking for something more exciting."

"Sorry to hear that," he said rolling his tongue between his lips.

"That's okay," she said. "Have you got a girlfriend?"

"No," he said.

"That surprises me," she said.

"Why does it surprise you?" he asked.

"Well you're very good looking. You could pull ducks out of water," she said, feeling the rush of blood filling her cheeks.

"I don't know how to take that," he said.

"That's how I see you," she said. "In my eyes you are very attractive."

Brady couldn't think of having ever received any compliments at all in his life. He had been used to suffering criticism so the words coming out of Myra's mouth had been quite unexpected.

The sound of the siren blowing, indicating that the break was over, jolted her from the hypnotic trance she had fallen under by the sound of his Scottish accent.

She was over the moon. Clasping her hands together tightly she skipped back into the office like a child in a sweet shop.

With the help of Bert her plan had worked. She had broken the ice. She was now convinced that she had claimed her prize and got Brady more than interested in her.

Brady, on the other hand, had also got his own plans for her.

CHAPTER TWO

The year was nearing its end and the office Christmas party was going to be a special one this time because the long serving Bert Matthews was retiring and Brady would be taking his place.

Myra had been dancing to You Were Made for Me by Freddie and The Dreamers and as she went to sit down, after the song ended, Brady walked unsteadily towards her.

"Do you want to dance?" he asked swaying backwards and forwards.

Nodding, and spilling her drink, she took his hand. They slowly danced around the room bumping against other people.

Brady hadn't a clue how to dance. He was very tipsy and kept stepping on her feet.

"Do you want to meet up for a few drinks after the party?" he asked.

"That's a good idea," she replied.

They met up later and went to a local pub near to where she lived.

He wanted to impress her. Standing up and slurring his words he sang, "Ying tong, ying tong, ying tong, ying tong, ying tong iddle I po, ying tong, ying tong, ying tong ying tong, ying tong iddle I po."

Giggling and hiccupping she said, "You sound like one of the Goons. I see you have a funny side to you."

"When I'm drunk; if I'm drunk," he said. "I act stupid and clumsy."

13

In their drunken state they never realized how quickly the evening had passed.

He walked her back home.

"Can I come in?" he asked.

"No," she replied. "Gran might still be up."

He grabbed her into his arms. His lips brushed against hers. Not innocently like a tease, but hot, fiery, passionate and demanding.

She pushed him away. Then she pulled his head gently towards her and tenderly kissed him. The only thing between them was the cold breeze that hit her face and made her heart dance.

Stepping back she said, "I think you'd better go."

"You don't know how long I've wanted to do this," he said.

She went inside the house, her heart pounding like a drum, and knew that her relationship with him had begun.

The festive season was over. Myra was looking forward to a new year and a new and exciting relationship with the man she had won over. Ian Brady had become her obsession. A prize she wasn't going to let go of.

The working day was almost at an end when Brady asked, "Do you fancy going to the flicks tonight?"

"That would be great," she replied. "King of Kings is showing and I've wanted to see it for ages."

"Okay," he said. "I'll come and pick you up at seven."

After almost three hours of sitting watching a boring movie, in Brady's opinion, they left the cinema.

The only interesting part of being in the cinema was that he had bought Myra bag of Butter Kist.

When he leaned over to take a handful he deliberately touched her breasts. She didn't complain.

As they were walking home, "Why are you interested in that shit?" he growled.

"It's not shit," she replied. "I was brought up catholic and all that shit, as you put it, is based on real life."

"There's no God," he said. "The clergy invented God. They preach to people telling them to breed the way they should breed. They live by laws that were made thousands of years ago, and they fear the God they are taught is kind and loving. Perversion is the way a man thinks, the way he feels, the way he lives. People are like maggots. Small, blind worthless fish bait."

"How can you say that?" she asked. "Don't you have a faith?"

"My faith is the Devil," he replied. "When I was a teenager I saw this vision of a green demon. It followed me everywhere I went. It scared the shit out of me so I made a pact with the Devil. Once this pact had been made I never saw the demon again."

"A pact with the Devil?" she asked.

"Yes," he replied. "What has God done for you? I don't know why you go to church every Sunday. Only hypocrites go to church. Are you a hypocrite?"

"No, I'm not," she replied. "I'll stop going just to please you."

"You don't have to please me," he said.

"Okay then," she said. "I'll stop going to prove I'm no hypocrite."

Turning into Bannock Street, "Look," she said. "The house is in darkness. That means gran has gone to bed. She usually goes to bed at around eight thirty. You can come in and I'll make us a brew."

She opened the door quietly and they both went inside.

They went into the front room and as she was taking off her coat he suddenly pushed her onto the couch.

She pulled him on top of her and her hot lips covered his mouth with a hungry kiss.

He reacted by sinking his teeth into her neck drawing her blood as he sank them deeper.

Quickly grabbing a cushion she bit on it to stifle her groans. She didn't want to wake her gran up.

Tearing at her blouse, like a dog on heat, he started biting her breasts. His hands, meanwhile, were frantically fumbling with her skirt until he pulled her underwear down.

"Turn over on your belly," he said. "I'm going to take you from behind."

As she lay face down he thrust deep into her arse.

She bit harder on the cushion as he continued thrusting deep inside her.

Within a few minutes it was all over. Not satisfied with buggering her he finally urinated inside her.

He rolled off her and lay on his back panting.

"That was the best fuck I've had," he said. "Now turn over and lie on your back."

She quickly turned over.

Her only desire was to admire his penis and beg for penetration.

This time she wasn't biting on the cushion. She was stifling her groans of pleasure by clutching his head to her face as he finally climaxed.

"That was brutal," she said as she sat up. "I'm bleeding from my arse and my fanny. Are you always like this with women? Are you a vampire?"

"My school friends used to call me Dracula. You're the first woman I've had sex with," he replied.

"My God," she said. "I've just been shagged by a virgin."

"Did I say I was a virgin?" he asked. "If the opportunity to perform one of these acts we've just performed presents itself, a man should take it."

"Let's go into the kitchen," she said. "I'll make us that brew before you go home."

"No. It's late," he said. "I should go home. I'll see you tomorrow at work."

Their relationship was developing and Brady was starting to reveal the true nature of his secret fantasies to her.

"I don't have much sexual experience," he said. "It's not that I don't want sex, it's because I find that what I want is hard to get."

"What do you mean by that?" she asked.

"I used to have violent thoughts when I was a teenager at school," he replied. The other boys had cards with pornographic pictures on them. I had far better pictures in my head. When I read the Marquis de Sade for the first time it was like looking in the mirror. You're the first person I've been able to talk to about this."

"When we had sex for the first time you made me think that you were a virgin," she said. "Your words were: did I say I was a virgin? I didn't know what you meant by that."

"I played around with other lads. You know just out of curiosity. We'd toss each other off. I only fucked one once." Her eyes fell to the floor as she asked, "So you like men as well as women?"

"I didn't say that," he snapped. "I told you I'd dabbled with other boys. You have to try other things. Don't knock what you haven't tried. If you don't like it, that's your problem. I am who I am and nothing, or anybody, will ever change me. Take it or leave it."

"I've got a secret to tell you too," she said. "And you can take it or leave it."

"What secret?" he asked.

"When I was fifteen I went to live in London," she said. "I got raped by an older man and had a baby daughter."

"What happened to her?" he asked.

"I dunno," she replied. "I gave her away when she was born and came back to live here."

"Fucking lying bitch," he said.

"Well I was no virgin either when you fucked me," she said. "So take that!"

17

He had got to know Myra very well and could see that she was obsessed with him. Whatever he told her she would never let him go. He wasn't particularly interested in her story. The world revolved around him. He believed she was

making it up for attention. He was testing the water with her and it was working.

"If you love me as much as you say you do then you won't question me. I don't really think you love me as much as you say," he said.

"I love you more than you realise," she said.

"Okay. Let's prove it," he said. "Would you do anything for me?"

"Anything," she replied. "I'd go to hell and back for you."

"You don't need to do that," he said. "Can I take some pornographic pictures of you? You know like the ones the Marquis of Sade would approve of?"

"Yes you can," she replied.

"Come on then let's go upstairs to your bedroom," he said. "Your gran's watching Coronation Street with your mum so they won't know what's going on."

They entered the bedroom and she locked the door behind her.

"Get me two pairs of your stockings," he said taking off his clothes.

She gave him what he'd asked for and stripped off and lay on the bed.

Tying her wrists, first to the top of the bed, he started fondling her breasts. His coarse tongue licked its way down her body until it reached her feet. He tied her ankles to the bottom of the bed. He removed his clothes and fell on top of her. He was penetrating her deeply and his hips were moving up and down like a fiddlers elbow. He bit all of her body until it was covered in burst blood vessels. When he had finished he got his camera and took snapshots of her tied to the bed.

He untied her and said, "Now crouch down on the bed and look up at the camera. Did you enjoy that?"

"I did," she replied. "That kind of sex excites me."

"That's good to hear," he said. "You've made me happy by saying that because you can help me realise my fantasies."

They both got dressed.

Beckoning her he said, "Come over here. I have something for you."

Holding her close to him he bit her hard on the cheekbone, just below her right eye, until her face began to bleed.

Trying to fight him off she screamed, "What the fuck was that for?"

"That's for accepting a lift from another work mate," he replied laughing. "Never, and I mean never, accept a lift from him again."

Going downstairs he turned to her like a male stripper without charm and said, "I suggest you stay off work tomorrow the state your face is in."

He left.

She went into the front room where her gran and mother were watching TV.

"Oh my God," said her gran standing up and then quickly slumping back onto the couch. "What happened to you?"

"Has he done this to you?" Myra's mother asked. "You know that I can't stand the creep. He's no good for you and never will be. He's about as useful as an ashtray on a motorbike. I don't know what you see in him. I wish he'd get lost."

"Ian and me went to the pub round the corner. There was a fight and I was hit by a flying beer bottle," she replied.

They both looked at her open mouthed. Who could blame them?

CHAPTER 3

One weekend after they had been living together for a few weeks Brady said, "I know we've been talking a lot about doing a bank job but I've had another idea. I want to commit the perfect murder."

"What?" Myra asked.

"The perfect murder," he replied. "I found a book about a couple of rich yanks who thought they had committed the perfect murder but they cocked it all up. I know that we can do it without being caught and I have the perfect plan."

"And what plan might that be?" she asked.

"We have to rehearse everything until we get it perfect," he replied. "You can drive me around the neighbourhood and we'll observe some kids."

"Kids?" she asked. "Why kids?"

"Kids are easier to pick up," he replied. "You are a woman and kids trust women more than they trust men. It will be as easy as pie."

"I don't know," she said. "I don't know if I could do it."

Grabbing her by the throat, "You have to do it," he said scrunching his nose and showing his teeth. "You promised you'd do anything for me and this is easier than going to hell and back."

"Okay, okay," she said pushing him away from her. "Let's go and drive around the neighbourhood."

"One more thing," he said. "I've been reading a lot in the local paper about folks around here badly treating their pets. They're going to pay for it. I've noted down some addresses. Tonight, when it's dark, we'll go and hurl some bricks through their windows. The bastards. I hate twats who are cruel to animals."

"This book you found," she asked. "Why did they cock up the murder?"

"They were seen by people who knew them," he replied.

"They didn't clean up after them and they hid the body in a drainage pipe with a foot sticking out. When we commit the perfect murder we'll make sure that the body is never found."

They were driving around the neighbourhood. Brady saw a group of young boys playing football.

"Stop the car here," he said. "Let me take some photos. I'll develop them in the dark room back home."

They waited for it to get dark. She drove him to the addresses he'd noted down of those responsible for treating their animals with cruelty. He hurled rocks through the windows. Myra drove off faster than God on a skateboard before they could get caught.

He came looking for her early the next morning.

"It's a beautiful Sunday morning," he said. "I fancy taking a drive onto the moors. Do you have time or are you going to church?"

"I thought I'd made it clear to you that I'm not going to church anymore," she replied.

"Fine," he said. "Then we'll go to the moors. We can spend the day there."

"I'll ask gran if she'd like to come with us," she said.

"No," he grunted. "We're going alone. I've got plans I need to talk about. Those

plans are between you and me. The old bat will have to stay here."

"Okay," she said. "I'll go and make some sandwiches. Go and wait in the car. Here are the keys. And don't call my gran an old bat."

Myra was very fond of her gran and wouldn't have anything bad said about her. Her gran idolized her and Myra could twist her round her little finger.

Cheese and ham sandwiches made, accompanied by a flask of tea, they headed for the moors.

After twenty minutes of driving out of the city the woods gave way to sparse moorland and soon they could see the giant granite rocks rising out of the waving sea of rough grass.

"Pull up here in this layby," he said. "This looks like a good spot for a picnic."

They got out of the car and walked onto the moor. The peat shifted under their feet as they stepped on it. It was like walking on packets of marshmallows.

They walked a few hundred yards. Over the brow of the hill a lake appeared as if by magic. It shone like a mirror in the sun and was shaped like a perfectly flat disc of metal. No sound rang out from the emptiness of the space they were in. The whiff of heather wafted up their noses. The place was as still as a vault. The only sounds were the echo of a crow.

"This place reminds me of Scotland," Brady said. "Here among nature and at peace. A good place to hide bodies."

She laid the woollen blanket, that she had taken from the car, down on the ground.

Sitting down on the blanket he said, "Now I'll tell you about our plans."

"Our plans?" she asked.

"You're not getting cold feet are you?" he asked.

"I'm still not sure about this," she replied. "If we kill somebody and get caught they will hang us."

"We're not going to get caught," he said. "I told you we are going to commit the perfect murder. They'll never find a body up here. That's why we're here."

"So you're going to bring them up here and bury them?" she asked.

"Just listen to what I have planned," he replied. "You will wear a disguise. A wig. We'll look for a child and you will go over and speak to them."

"A child?" she asked. "Why a child? And why me?"

"A child will be easier to pick up," he replied. "A young kid will confide more in you than they will in a man. Parents always warn their kids not to talk to strange men. They don't tell them not to talk to strange women. Once we've got the
kid we'll bring it up here, torture it, kill it and bury it."

You'll pick it up in the car. I'll follow you on my motorbike and when I see someone I want, I'll flash my headlight three times. That'll be your signal to pull up and ask them to help you. You'll drive up here with them and I'll follow on my bike."

"How are you going to bury them?" she asked.

"I'll put a shovel in the back of the car so we can dig a grave," he replied. "Look here," he said, taking a lump of peat in his hand. "The ground is soft and easy to dig. It won't take long. Then we'll drive home and clean everything up after. We can't leave anything to chance. I am going to commit the perfect murder and you are going to help me."

"What are we going to say to the child?" she asked.

"I'm thinking about that one," he replied. "Don't worry I'll think of something. But we have to practise every step before it's done."

They had the picnic and sat talking for hours.

"Got it," he said. "Once we have the kid you can tell it you lost something and ask them if they'll help you look for it. You can offer them something in exchange like some sweets or some money. They'll jump at that."

"Give me some time to think about it," she said.

Pinching her arm and glaring at her he said, "Well don't take too long in thinking about it. Now let's have a practice run."

He pulled her up and hauled her over his shoulders like a sack of potatoes.

Walking as best he could with her he stumbled on the rocks and she fell to the ground.

"What the fuck do you think you're playing at?" she cried.

"I need to practise carrying a dead body up here," he laughed.

"Well I'm not fucking dead," she said.

The sun had started to sink behind the hills in the distance painting the sky shades of pink and red. They had been on the moor all day.

"Looks like it's time to go home," she said and they walked back to the car.

They got home drank some wine and went to bed.

She raised her heavy eyelids half way only for them to fall shut. She raised them again and swung her bare feet to the floor again.

Once on her feet the room swayed almost causing her to lose balance and she reached out for the wall. Her hand slipped and she sprawled onto the floor with a crashing thump. The room swirled before becoming stationary again. She used the bed to pull herself up. Her stomach turned in an unfriendly way.

She couldn't remember drinking that much wine the night before.

She looked at the clock. It was one in the afternoon.

It looked as if she had slept with all of her clothes on. They were unbuttoned and twisted awkwardly around her body.

She pulled herself together and went downstairs.

"Why didn't you go to work today chuck?" her gran asked.

"I don't feel too good gran," she replied. "I have a terrible migraine. I think it was being out on the moor all day yesterday. I think the cold air brought it on."

"When you go up there," her gran said. "Make sure you are wrapped up warm. You should know it's a lot colder up there than down here."

She felt groggy for the rest of the day and it was only when Brady returned from work that she realized what had happened.

"Did you sleep well last night?" he asked.

"I can't understand why I slept till one this afternoon and I still feel bad. What did you say to them at work when I didn't show up?"

"Nobody asked," he replied. "I'm your boss and they know we live together. It's none of their business anyway. So they wouldn't ask me, would they?"

"I only drank that one glass of wine last night," she said. "I can't understand why I've got a hangover."

"You haven't got a hangover," he said calmly. "I slipped some of your gran's sleeping tablets in your wine. I took some pornographic snaps of you while you were out cold. Naked and close up."

"What for?" she asked.

"I'll make it clear," he replied. "I'm in control and you'll do exactly what I want, or else. I hope you've made up your mind because I have everything in place."

But she was still not quite ready.

Frustrated, Brady asked, "Is there anyone you hate so much that you'd like to see them dead?"

She thought about it for a while.

"Yes. As a matter of fact there is."

He hopped up and down like a little girl. His eyes lit up. "Who?" he asked.

"Pauline Reade," she replied.

"Who the fuck is Pauline Reade?" he asked.

"She's David Smith's ex," she replied. "You know. Maureen's boyfriend?"

"Why do you want her dead?" he asked.

"She's a threat to Maureen," she replied. "The cunt lives a door away from Dave and I still think she fancies him. I think she's trying to cause problems between them."

"Are you nominating her as our first victim?" he asked.

"Yes I am," she replied without blinking an eye.

In this instant she had confirmed to Brady that she was ready to kill. She had made up her mind.

CHAPTER 4

"We have to go to the moor and prepare it before we kill her," said Brady.

"What do you mean?" asked Myra. "Prepare the moor."

"I'm going to offer you to the Devil," he replied. "Then that ground will be sacred for us to bury our victims there. I'll buy a compass and ceremonial dagger from the army and navy stores in the city. You can buy some black candles. You

will have to practise the notes I have written down by heart."

That night Brady showed her the dagger he had bought.

"Look at this," he said pulling it from its black nylon sheath. "It's a beauty, isn't it?"

"Are you going to kill Pauline with that?" she asked.

"We need this for the ceremony tomorrow night," he replied, holding the black, cast metal handle and gently sliding a finger down the double edged blade. "This knife can pierce a rib cage."

"I'll ask you again then," she said. "Are you going to kill Pauline with it?"

"Wait and see," he replied.

The moonlight bathed them in its silvery glow. It lit the moor from pitch black to smoky grey. In the distance the craggy rocks of Hollin Brown Knoll were silhouetted against the deep sky.

"Right," he said. "Let's get started. We need to look for something we can use as an altar. It has to face the north."

"How about this?" said Myra pointing to a clump of rocks."

"Those look good," he replied. "We can place them on top of one another. Let's check the compass and see if they are facing in the right direction."

Shining his torch onto the compass, "We need to position them a little bit over there," he said.

They arranged the rocks and formed a makeshift altar.

He placed a drawing he had sketched of the Devil on it. She gently placed three black candles on top of it making sure they wouldn't fall off.

"It's almost midnight," he said. "Time to get starkers."

They quickly removed all of their clothes and lay them on the ground.

"Light the candle," he said and turned off his torch. "Now we're facing north so close your eyes. I'll count to three and we'll start the banishing. "One, two, three."

Together they chanted, "I focus my mind and my will upon the Prince of Darkness," nine times.

"Now," Brady said. "We'll recite the general invocation. Ready after three. One, two, three."

"Hail unto my Master, the Devil, the lord of this world and Prince of Darkness! The red one of the darkest brilliance, whose eternal shadow is the light of my life. Surely I belong to thee in both body and spirit. I have taken thy name as a part of myself and I rejoice in thy spirit. For in the shadow of Lucifer there is love and warmth, and in the midst of his darkness there is undying light. O mighty black goat of the wilderness! O mighty serpent of Eden's demise! To thee I give praise forever and ever. Amen. Master, I call thee forth from the bottomless abyss. Master, I call thee forth from the ends of the earth. Master, I call thee forth from the night time sky. Come forth from within my flesh and my spirit and greet me as thy humble servant and friend. I wish to worship and honour thee, to commune with thee and to be still and know that thou art my God."

The dagger glistened in the moonlight. He pointed it northward into the air. Tracing a pentagram he said, "Oh hear the names of the mighty Prince of Darkness!

Hail to thee, Belial, god of this world! Lord of the Earth and Spirit of the flesh. He whose strength is in the mountain. Help me to be strong and to embrace the pleasures and pains of earthly existence. All praise unto thee, Lord Belial! Hail

Belial!"

Turning to the northwest and tracing another pentagram in the air he said,

"Hail to thee, Behemoth, beast of the Earth! Lord of the waters and the Earth, great beast of revelation! He whose voice is the call of the wild. Help me to be the best and most successful animal that I can be. All praise unto thee, Lord Behemoth! Hail Behemoth!"

He turned and faced the west. Tracing another pentagram in the air he said,

"Hail to thee, Typhon, beast of the sea! Lord of the waters and creature of the depths. He who is the heart of the thunderous hurricane. Help me to understand the deepest regions of myself, and to be a raging storm against all that would oppress me. All praise unto thee, Lord Typhon! Hail Typhon!"

He then turned around to face the southwest. He traced another pentagram in the air saying, "Hail to thee, Set, great red dragon! Lord of the flame and the waters, outsider-god. He who roams the lonely wilderness. Help me to stay true to myself, and to overcome all that would infringe upon my selfhood. All praise unto

thee, Lord Set! Hail Set!"

Rotating his position he turned facing the south and traced another pentagram in the air.

"Hail to thee, Shaitan, adversary! Lord of the flame and supreme enemy of the God of Abraham. He who left the Kingdom of Heaven in flames. Help me to always remain strong in the face of the tyrant God, and to prevail over my enemies! All praise unto thee, Lord Shaitan. Hail Shaitan!"he said.

He moved and faced to the southeast. Tracing another pentagram in the air he said, "Hail to thee, Samael, serpent of Eden! Lord of the air and the flame, venomous one. He who tempted Adam and Eve with the fruit of knowledge. Help me to find and maintain the strength to think for myself, and to do what I

know in my heart is right. All praise unto thee, Lord Samael! Hail Samael!"

Turning and facing the east and tracing another pentagram in the air, "Hail to thee, Lucifer, bringer of light! Lord of the air and morning star. He who destroys ignorance with the calling of the dawn. Help me to pierce through my own blindness and to find the light of understanding. All praise unto thee, Lord

Lucifer! Hail Lucifer!"

He moved his body again and faced the northeast. He traced another pentagram in the air saying, "Hail to thee, Azazel, scapegoat! Lord of the Earth and

the air, dark horned god. He whose celestial knowledge is drawn to the earth by worldly lust. Help me to achieve knowledge and happiness here on earth and in the flesh. All praise unto thee, Lord Azazel! Hail Azazel!"

Finally he'd turned full circle and was facing the north.

He put the dagger down on the ground and raised both his hands into the air making the sign of the Devil's horns.

"Hail to thee, Prince of Darkness! Lord of the elements, beloved Master! He who is of the darkness, but who brings the light. Help me to serve you in as many ways that I can. All praise unto thee, my Prince of Darkness! Hail Satan! Hail

Set!"

He fell to his knees bowing his head towards the north. He remained silent for two minutes.

He got up and said, "Master, I believe in thee. Master, I pass near to thee! Thou art in my flesh. Thou art in my blood, and thou art in my very soul. Thy spirit gives refreshment to me when I am thirsty. Thy spirit heals me when I am sick. Thou make me to search for the hidden answers. Thou make me to be wise. Forever am I indebted to thee my Lord and muse. I live for thee and I breathe for thee. I pass into being for thee. Hail Lucifer, the lord and prince of this world!"

In the candle light Myra's features looked sharp. Her skin mellow like a peach. She looked so different. In this light she could be anyone, but she wasn't. She was Myra, the accomplice.

"Now we have to make the sacrificial offering," he said. "Give me your hand."

He pricked her thumb with the point of the dagger. Then he pricked his own thumb.

He rubbed his thumb on hers allowing their blood to mix.

"Lie down," he said. "I'm going to fuck you."

Her painted toes dug into the spongy peat. As he thrust inward all she could see was his face and the moon above.

Entering her again and again and again. She let out moans of ecstasy.

His body shuddered. His muscles tightened as he climaxed. It was over.

"Now we'll pray," he said.

He'd written a short prayer on a piece of paper.

She reached for her bag and gave him the piece of paper.

In the torch light they both read.

"We pray asking that we will be able to find peace and happiness."

"Now it's time to give thanks," he said.

Together they prayed.

"I give thanks unto thee, Prince Lucifer my Master. For all that thou hath done for me. I give thanks unto thee for guiding me, for giving me strength in my hour of

darkness, and for never leaving my side. Thou art truly a most noble and loving God, and to thee I am forever devoted in both spirit and flesh."

"We have to close the ritual by reciting the closing hymn," he said.

They both spoke the hymn which he had got her to rehearse.

"I hear you calling from inside my soul. My mind is opened to occluded sight like black lightning without control. In my heart your thunder dwells pushing and pulling me to the dark. With you in me my humanity swells. An animal with my Master's mark. Guide me oh night spirit of the wild, who leads me and loves me as his child. Teach me, oh wise one of the tower, who nurtures thought, the sacred power. Lead me to the sacred tree! Light the spark that is dark as night! Open the gates to the left hand path! O beloved Azazel, my bringer of light!"

In the silence they heard the sound of a sudden wind sweeping across the moor.

A draught swirled up from where they had been lying, thrusting out into the night sky. Snatches of cold air licked their feet. Even the candles shook in fright as they blew themselves out.

Evil was rubbing its hands over them.

CHAPTER 5

The early evening summer sky cloaked the cobbled streets. It was an ordinary evening. The cotton bud clouds moved lazily across the sky. The sun gleamed brightly forcing them to squint and stare down.

"Right Hessy," Brady said turning to Myra. "Let's start hunting. Tonight we are going to commit the perfect murder."

He had given her the pet name Hessy after Rudolf Hess, Hitler's deputy Fuhrer.

"Let me look at you," he said.

She was wearing a light, checked beige coat, a pair of black slacks, black shoes, a beige blouse and a pair of black shiny gloves. Her bleached blonde hair was covered with a black cotton headscarf.

Counting the buttons on her coat Brady carefully looked her up and down.

"Perfect," he said. "Remember what I told you. Drive slowly around the neighbourhood. When you see me flash my headlight that's the signal for you to pull over and offer that person a lift. Understand?"

"Yes," she replied as she got into the van.

She was driving down Gorton Lane. Glancing into the rear view mirror she saw the signal. She continued driving and passed a young girl who was walking in the opposite direction.

Brady drew up alongside the car on his motorbike and ordered her to stop.

"What the fuck is going on?" he said banging his fist on the car door. "Why didn't you stop and pick her up?"

"I know that girl," she replied. "It's Marie Ruck. She lives next door to my mother."

"Well let's get on with the fucking hunt then," he said.

She continued driving around and had just turned into Wiles Street when she saw Pauline Reade leaving her house.

Pauline wasn't a girl anymore and she never would be again. She was sweet sixteen and wouldn't have looked out of place in a school uniform.

She was wearing a pink party frock under a pale blue coat. Her white high heeled shoes matched the gloves she was carrying.

Myra's heart fluttered. She pulled up and rolled down the window.

"Hiya Pauline," she said. "You look dolled up. Where are you going?"

"I'm going to a dance at the Railway Club," she replied. "I knocked on Dave's door to see if your Maureen wanted to come but there's nobody in. I don't fancy going by myself."

"Our Mo has probably gone round to gran's house," Myra said. "I tell you what. Jump in and I'll give you a lift. We can see if she's there."

"Thanks," she said.

Getting into the car she hadn't noticed that one of her gloves had fallen out of her hand into the gutter below.

When they arrived at gran's house Myra got out of the car.

"Wait here, Pauline," she said. "I'll go and see if our Mo is inside."

Myra was in and out of the house in a flash.

"No," she said. "She isn't with gran. I don't know where she could be. She's

probably gone somewhere with Dave."

"Looks like I'll be going to the dance by myself then," said Pauline.

"Don't worry," she said. "I'll give you a lift so you don't have to walk."

"That's kind of you," she said. "If it's no trouble."

"No trouble at all," she said. "Will you do me a favour?"

"What's that?" she asked.

"I lost an expensive glove on the moor. Ian bought me a pair for my birthday last year. He's gone raving mad and I need to find it. It isn't eight o'clock yet. We can drive up there and look for it and then I can take you to the dance after. It won't take long."

Pointing to a pile of records in the back of the van Myra continued.

"I'll give you some gramophone records. Will you give me a hand?"

"Of course," she replied.

Meanwhile, Brady had been waiting and had been wondering what Myra was up to.

The car pulled away from gran's house and Brady followed.

They were approaching the moor.

"Why are you nervous Myra?" asked Pauline.

"I'm not nervous," she replied. "What makes you think I'm nervous?"

"You're gripping the steering wheel very tightly," she replied.

"Well Pauline," she said. "We're getting near the moor and you never know if a sheep or other animal will come darting out in front of the car. I'd never forgive myself if anything happened to you."

They reached the moor at about eight thirty. Brady was waiting for them in a layby.

Myra had noticed that Pauline was wearing a gold locket and chain.

They got out of the car and Brady approached them.

"This is my boyfriend Ian," Myra said introducing Pauline to Brady. "Ian, this is Pauline."

"Our little helper," he said.

The summer breeze fluttered around caressing everything it touched. The air was filled with the perfume of heather as they walked on the moor.

The layby disappeared as they walked over the brow of the hill.

"That's a nice locket," Myra said, quickly snatching it from Pauline's neck. "You won't need it where you're going."

"What are you doing Myra?" she asked, as her heart started to pound.

"I know you still fancy Dave," she replied. "He is Mo's boyfriend now and all of this is going to stop."

Brady and Myra dragged her to the ground and started to remove her clothing.

She twisted and turned trying to escape their clutches but had no chance with both of them on top of her.

Myra stuck two of her fingers in Pauline's vagina while Brady held her down.

When she was sexually satisfied Brady sliced into Pauline's throat twice with the dagger they had used at the ritual.

"I'll go and get the shovel from the car," he said. "You wait here with her."

The peat absorbed the blood seeping from Pauline's wounds creating an irregular stain that would eventually be washed away by the summer rain leaving it to go unnoticed.

Myra looked down at her. She was still alive.

A few minutes later Brady returned with the spade.

Myra's breath was shaking and getting rapid. The blood was pounding in the back of her head. Her hands clutching her slacks.

"She's still alive," she said.

"We'll soon put a stop to that," he said. "Give me your headscarf."

He took the headscarf and pulled it tightly around Pauline's throat. The gurgling sound stopped. It was all over.

He stepped aside and went and dug the grave.

When he'd finished digging he dropped his pants and said, "She's not going to feel this." He raped her.

They dragged her body and dumped it in the shallow grave.

The night was slowly eating the day. The warm sunlight was being swallowed by the horizon. Twinkling spotlights were now adorning the sky.

Myra looking into the darkness said, "This is the night Pauline Reade died, my soul died and God died."

Walking away from the grave Brady took hold of her arm and said, "If you'd shown any signs of backing out you'd have ended up in the same hole."

"I know," she said.

They loaded the motorbike into the back of the van and returned home from the moor.

They drove past Pauline's mum and brother who were searching the streets for her.

Inside the house Brady counted the buttons on Myra's coat and his coat and also on his shirt. He had to make sure that Pauline hadn't torn anything from them in the frenzied struggle for her life.

Myra filled a bucket with hot soapy water and they both went outside.

Brady immaculately washed the van inside and out.

Myra hissed, "Why are you washing the fucking tyres?"

"We have to make sure that everything is spotlessly clean," he replied.

They made a fire in the yard and burned the clothes they had been wearing and returned inside the house.

Myra sat down on the sofa. Brady approached her with a bottle of Drambuie he had purchased earlier that day.

"After all the years of dreaming about the perfect murder I've actually done it," he said. "How do you feel about it?"

"Never in my wildest dreams did I think that anything like this could ever happen," she replied crying.

"Here," he said pouring her a glass of Drambuie. "Drink this."

Putting his arm around her shoulder and kissing her clumsily on the cheek. "It's all over now," he said. "You'll learn to live with it. I'll try and control my temper. I won't hit or hurt you anymore."

Still crying and clinging to him, "I'll do everything I can to cope with what's happened," she said. "I'll do my best not to irritate you."

Her heart flooded with the love and emotions that she had felt for him for so long as he gently stroked her hair.

CHAPTER SIX

It had been eleven days since they had murdered Pauline. Myra was celebrating her twenty first birthday.

Brady strutted into the office. He placed the neatly wrapped packet onto the desk where she was sitting, pushing it closer to her. She peered down. His arms crossed over his chest.

She looked up at him, not knowing exactly what he was going to say. The corners of his mouth were turned up in one of his grins, the pride radiating off of him, almost tangible.

"Happy Birthday," he said. "Go on open it."

"Let me guess what it is," she said picking it up and shaking it. "I don't know what it could be. It looks like I'll have to open it."

Pulling at the wrapping and taking care not to tear it, she opened the box that was inside. Opening her mouth and placing one hand over it she gasped as she saw the gold – plated Ingersoll wristwatch.

"Ian," she said. "You shouldn't have bought me this."

"Don't you like it?" he asked.

"Of course I like it," she replied. "I don't want you to go spending your money on things like this."

"You're only twenty one once," he said. "And you deserve it."

"Okay," she said. "We'll go to the pub tonight and I'll pay for the drinks."

"I have a better idea," he said. "On Sunday we'll have a bar meal for lunch at the Huntsman and invite Maureen and David. They allow dogs inside so you can bring Puppet. I'll bring a couple of bottles of wine and we can drink them later

on the moor."

The stark, stone building stood like a monument above the shimmering haze of the city.

Walking into the inn was like stepping back in time. One could have imagined bumping into Robin Hood and his Merry Men sitting there drinking ale. The only thing lacking were spittoons. Old beer tankards were hanging haphazardly above the wooden bar. Cigarette smoke gracefully danced its way upwards, in grey ghostly wisps, to the low wooden beamed ceiling, until it found its way out through the open windows and into the fresh air outside.

It was crowded and noisy. The smell from the Sunday roast was doing its best to disguise the odour of cigarettes and beer. The patrons chatted noisily among themselves as they clanked their glasses on the wooden tables. There was

the sound of darts as they landed on the dartboard and then a whoop of triumph from one man while the others groaned.

Brady walked up to the bar as the others walked through the room and out into the beer garden at the back.

"There are four of us here for lunch," he said to the barman. "We're going to take a table outside. Would you mind sending someone to take our order?"

"You have to order here," the barman replied. "The waitress will bring the meals to your table."

"Right," Brady said. "Four Sunday roasts and a bottle of Liebfraumilch."

"Thank you sir," the barman said. "The waitress will be with you shortly."

An elderly gentleman, carrying a glass of beer, wasn't looking where he was going when he walked past their table.

He accidentally trod on the dog and splashed beer over them, soaking Brady's shirt.

"Watch it, mate!" Brady said in irritation.

The man's face flushed red as he saw Brady's wet shirt.

"I do apologise," the man said with a trembling voice.

Brady stood up and was about to thump him in the face but realising he was an old man he sat down again.

"No worries," Brady said. "I'll get you another."

"No need," the man said, shrugging his shoulders, and walked away.

Three hours later, Brady, Myra, Maureen, and David found themselves on the moor.

"Hey Dave," Brady said. "Let's go for a stroll."

"Okay," he said.

"The women can talk about women's things," said Brady. "We can talk men's talk."

Brady was clever. He wanted to take the opportunity of getting David on his own.

David always tried to portray himself as a tough guy. Instead his insecurity always got the better of him. He wasn't homosexual but had an inclination towards men. He saw something in Brady, who was ten years older than him, but couldn't put his finger on it.

"You have a criminal record, don't you?" Brady asked.

"I have been in trouble in the past," David replied. "But they were petty things. Why do you ask?"

"I've been thinking about doing a bank job," he replied. "But I need somebody to help. I think you would be the best choice."

"Does Myra know about this?" he asked.

"She's going to drive the getaway car," he replied. "I spent time in the nick when I was younger. It was before I came to live in Manchester."

"What for?" he asked.

"Robbery," he replied. "I murdered a bloke as well and dumped him in the canal. But I got away with that."

Stopping in his tracks and taking Brady by the arm. "You killed somebody?" he asked.

"Yes," he replied showing no emotion. "Murder is a hobby and a supreme pleasure. We come from nothing. We go to nothing. The only thing in between is here and now. Murder is an existential experience."

"Oh my God," said David.

"Why do you say oh my God?" Brady asked. "God is a disease, a plague, a disease which eats away man's instincts. God is a superstition. You are your own master. You live for one thing. Supreme pleasure in everything you do. I've murdered more than once."

His heart pounding, David stopped in his tracks. The only sound he could hear

was the sound of his own pulse throbbing in his ears. Each second seemed to play on forever as he was following in the footsteps of his likely killer. He didn't feel safe being alone with Brady and said, "Let's go back and join the women."

"We need to talk about the bank job first," he said. "I've got some guns."

"You're going to use guns?" he asked.

"We need guns," he replied. "We don't have to use them."

What happens if the bank tries to raise the alarm?" asked David.

"We run out of the bank," he replied.

"You have to shoot before the police have the chance to come," he said.

"We don't have to shoot to kill," David said.

"You're a yellow belly, aren't you?" Brady asked.

"No I'm not," he replied.

"I've got a bank in mind," said Brady. "It's the one on Hyde Road. I want you to go there and observe the comings and goings. Take notes. Do you understand?"

Nodding his head, David said, "I have to take a piss. I'll go over there."

"I need one too," said Brady. "I'll come with you."

"Why do you want to follow me?" he asked. "Are you queer?"

"I can think of other things to get pleasure from than sticking my prick up your arse." he replied.

Myra and Maureen had been chatting while the men were away.

"I'm ever so pleased that we're seeing more of each other," said Maureen. "I didn't see you much when you and Ian got together."

"Look, Mo," Myra said. "We're sisters and I won't allow anything to get in the way of that."

"I'm worried about you," Maureen said. "You've changed since you met Ian. You can be very surly at times. I'm not the only one who's noticed the change in you. You never used to be like that."

"We all change over time," Myra said.

"It's awful about Pauline disappearing," said Maureen. "I wonder what happened to her."

"She probably ran off with somebody," Myra replied. "You know what young kids are like these days. The swinging sixties where anything goes. They have no respect. All teenagers are rebels."

"I don't think Pauline was like that," she said. "She was a very quiet girl."

"She was David's ex, wasn't she?" Myra asked.

"It wasn't anything serious," she replied. "She had a crush on him. That's all."

"Well now she's not around she's no threat to you and Dave," Myra said.

"I never saw her as a threat," she said. "Look the boys are coming back."

"Have you finished your women's talk?" Brady asked.

"We have," replied Myra. "And have you finished your men's talk?"

"Correct," he replied. "Now we can finish off the rest of the wine and celebrate your birthday."

Brady took photos while David and the women were singing and dancing.

Little did David and Maureen realise that three feet below them lay the body of Pauline Read

CHAPTER SEVEN

Myra had been in some trouble with the police. She hadn't paid for the road tax for her van and had borrowed someone else's tax disc to use. They had spotted it and she had to appear at the magistrate's court.

House to house calls over the disappearance of Pauline Reade were still going on.

The front door knocked.

Myra opened the door and gaped when she saw his sharp jaw, chin, and cheekbones. His eyes were dark brown, shaped by bushy eyebrows. His soft thin lips were captivating and attractive.

"Good evening," he said. "I'm police constable Norman Sutton."

"Good evening," Myra replied.

"I understand you've had a bit of bother with us recently regarding your van. Do you want to keep it?" he asked. "A friend of mine has a business mending fridges and he needs something like it."

"Would you like a cup of tea?" she asked. "Come in and we can talk about it."

His soft lips stretched into a smile. "I don't have time right now," he said.

"Okay," she said. "I'll let you have the van."

"How much do you want for it?" he asked.

"Fifteen quid will do," she replied.

"That's giving it away," he said. "I tell you what I'll give you twenty five. I can't give you the cash though while I'm on duty. Could we perhaps meet up one evening for a drink and settle the deal?"

Brady had distanced himself from Myra after Pauline's murder and she had started to attend night school. They hadn't been seeing much of each other.

"Okay. I'll meet you after my night school class next Wednesday," she replied.

"Okay. It's a deal," he said. He got on his motorbike and rode off.

Norman was waiting outside the college as Myra was leaving her evening class.

"It's great to see you again," he said. "There's a pub just around the corner. We can go there."

Myra sipped on her rum and coke while he took a drink from his pint of beer.

"I remember you when you were working as a barmaid at Belle Vue," he said. "My mother was the manageress."

"Really?" she asked. "I never did have a good head for faces so I don't remember customers, but I remember your mam. It's a small world, isn't it?"

"Are you satisfied with twenty five pounds?" he asked, handing the crisp notes over to her."

"Yes. That's fine," she replied.

They finished their drinks and he took her home on his motorbike.

Her gran was in bed by now and there was no sign of Brady. She had found out that he was going to homosexual haunts.

"Come in Norman," she said. "I'll make some tea. If Ian shows up you'll have to pretend you've popped round with the money for the van and leave."

"Are you serious about Ian?" he asked.

"I am," she replied. "But there's a problem."

"What problem?" he asked.

"He said he never wants to get married or have kids," she replied.

"That's a bit hard," he said.

She made the tea and and poured him a cup.

Norman gently leaned toward her and kissed her warm lips, long and slowly.

They pulled apart and took shallow breaths.

"If Ian can play around why can't I," she thought. "But this man is married."

"Let's meet again after your next class," he said.

"Yes," she said. "I'd like that."

The following weekend she rented a car. She and Brady drove to Highfield Country Park on the outskirts of the city.

They were sitting on the grass eating sandwiches.

"I sold the van to a policeman," she said.

A laugh came from Brady like a leak stopping and starting. He rolled his eyes to the sky and bit on his upper lip. Suddenly he shook and his face grew tight as he let out a loud holler.

"We used that van to kill Pauline Reade," he laughed. "And you went and sold it to a cop."

Myra started to giggle as she could now see the funny side.

"I'm having an affair with him," she said. "And he's married."

"That's okay," he said putting a bottle of beer to his mouth. "I find it very amusing. But remember you still belong to me. Anyway, I'm having it off as well with another guy!"

Giving him the cold shoulder she continued munching on her sandwich.

She continued having her affair with Norman. The sexual relationship with him was like chalk and cheese compared to the sex she had been having with Brady. She

had to be honest with herself and knew that this new relationship was only temporary.

Brady had decided it was time he started seeing more of her again.

"Look what I've got for you," he said.

"It's 24 Hours from Tulsa," she replied.

"I'm sorry I haven't been seeing you as regular as you want and I want to make up for it. I know you like Gene Pitney. This is a peace offering."

"I'm seeing Norman tonight," she said.

"No problem," he said. "Just make sure it's the last time you see him or there'll be trouble. I'll tell his wife and his bosses at the cop shop what's going on between you two. Then I'll beat the fuck out of him."

"You wouldn't do that," she said.

"Wouldn't I?" he asked. "Try me."

That night after making love with Norman, she turned to him and said, "I'm sorry Norm but it's over."

"Why?" he asked.

"You're married and I've got Ian," she replied. "And I don't want to be part of a marriage break up. I have enough on my plate at the moment."

"What do you see in Ian?" he asked. "I can't understand."

"It's impossible to put into words," she replied.

While Myra had been having her sultry affair with the policeman, Brady had also been having an affair with a teenage boy.

He had made many visits to The Rembrandt bar in Manchester city centre. It was frequented by homosexuals.

Sitting in a dark corner and drinking a glass of wine, Brady was attracted, like a moth to a flame, to a seventeen year old young lad standing at the bar.

The youth was clad in a tight black t-shirt and jeans. His mannerisms were just different, making him stand out no matter where he was.

Brady wanted him. Not for keeps, just to play. He got up and went and stood next to him.

"Hi. My name's Ian," he said. "What's your name?"

"Eddie," the young man replied.

"Let me buy you a drink Eddie," Brady said. "What will it be?"

"A pint of bitter," he replied.

"Come and sit with me at that table over there," Brady said pointing to where he had left his unfinished glass of wine. "We can get to know each other."

Eddie picked up his beer and took it over to the table.

"How old are you Eddie?" Brady asked.

"Old enough," he replied.

"You don't look eighteen to me," he said.

"I told you I'm old enough," he replied.

"Old enough for what?" he asked.

"I think you know what I mean," he replied.

"I was attracted to you like a butterfly to nectar," Brady said. "You look kind of shy and sweet. When we've finished our drinks let's take a walk along the canal."

Brady was playing Russian roulette. He was not only buying alcohol for someone under age but now he wanted to have a sexual encounter with him.

"I'd like that," Eddie said. His smile was soft with a hint of femininity.

Being openly gay in the early sixties was still illegal and they had to be very careful.

They finished their drinks, left the bar and walked along the canal towpath.

"We'll do it under there," Brady said, as they got to an old stone bridge.

It was the kind of night even a feather would fall without drifting one way or the other.

"My trousers are getting tight," Brady said, rubbing his hand between his legs. "I've got a hard on."

Looking at him Eddie said, "Well you certainly weren't standing in the back row when they were giving those out," he himself aroused by now.

Eddie's right hand found its way into Brady's unzipped fly.

He took the erection in his hand and rhythmically pulled it up and down.

Brady's breathing became quicker and his hips rotated. He wanted more. He loosened his belt and opened his fly wider. Rolling his eyes and pressing his lips hard together he felt Eddie's warm hand pulling him faster.

Clenching his fists and clenching his buttocks, "I'm coming," he gasped. "I'm going to shoot my load."

He came in short, spasmodic bursts.

"That was much better than a do it yourself job," he sighed with relief.

He cleaned himself up with the bottom of his shirt, zipped up his trousers and fastened his belt.

Eddie rinsed the come from his hands in the canal.

Only a rat swimming past in the canal was oblivious of what had gone on.

They both went off in different directions along the towpath.

CHAPTER EIGHT

One weekend in November, just after Myra had passed her driving test, they were sitting watching Sunday Night at the London Palladium.

Brady calmly said, "I want to do another one.'"

"Another what?" she asked.

"Another murder. What did you think I meant?" he replied.

"I can't believe it," she said. "You told me you wanted to commit the perfect murder. You've done that. You told me it was all over and that I'd learn to live with it. Why, for God's sake do you want to do another one?"

"Because I just do," he replied. "I've been thinking about it for some time. I have a half formed plan. I'll tell you what you need to know when I feel you need to know."

"No," she said. "I'm not being involved in anything like that again."

"You are already involved," he said. "You can't turn the clock back and undo what you've already done."

Screaming and shouting she lurched for his throat but he grabbed hers first.

"You're going to help me again so get that into your head. Bruce Forsyth's catchphrase is 'I'm in charge.' It looks like he has the same one as me. What do you think I get out of doing what we've done?" he asked.

"Because you're in charge," she replied. "Having the power over someone's life and death."

"Good. You know where I'm coming from now," he said and left.

Twelve year old John Kilbride and his friend, John Ryan, were just coming out of the cinema in Ashton-Under-Lyne. It was five o'clock.

"Let's go to the market and earn some pocket money helping the stall holders pack up," said John Kilbride.

"Okay," the other John said.

After they had finished, John Ryan caught the bus home and left John Kilbride with a stall holder.

"Thanks for helping me clear up," said the stall holder. "Here's a bag of broken biscuits. I'm off."

Autumn's hand was lying heavily on the market place. The stall holders had packed up and gone home.

It was a cold grey afternoon in late November. The weather had changed. A vast blanket of white hung over the market place. Discarded sheets of newspaper clung to the pavement. The tops of buildings disappeared in the swirling

grey. The streets smelled damp.

The young boy however, seemed particularly pleased with the bag of broken biscuits. He swung it in windmill motions as he walked along the street. He stopped and leaned against a salvage bin and started tucking into them.

Looking on were Brady and Hindley. Myra had placed some cardboard boxes nearby.

She approached him. She had disguised herself by wearing a black wig.

"Can you help me carry some boxes to my car?" she asked. "I'm sure your parents will be worried about you being out in the fog. I'll give you a lift back home in the car. And I'll give you a bottle of sherry for helping me."

"Okay," he said.

He carried the boxes to the car.

Brady was waiting in the back of a Ford Anglia car that Hindley had hired.

John put the boxes in the car and asked, "Where's the bottle of sherry?"

"It's at my house," she replied. "We'll go there first and pick it up then I'll drive you home."

"Right," he said and got into the car.

"Hello little boy. What's your name?" Brady asked.

"John," he replied.

"John who?" asked Brady.

"John Kilbride, sir," he replied.

But instead of driving him to her house she headed out to the moor.

"Where are we going?" John asked.

"I lost an expensive glove on the moor and I have to try to find it before I take you home," she replied. "The glove wasn't mine. It was a friend's so I need to find it."

"I don't think you'll find it in this fog," John said.

"Oh I'm sure I will if you help me look for it," she said. "And remember I'm going to give you a bottle of sherry."

The moor had changed. The bracken was yellow and the heather was passing from bloom. There was a faint odour of wood smoke in the air.

"Let's go and look for this glove before it gets too dark," Brady said.

Myra was holding John's hand while Brady walked in front of them carrying a bottle of whiskey.

"I think I've found something," Brady shouted. "Come over here John."

John let go of Myra's hand and ran to Brady who pushed him to the ground. He then threw himself on top of him.

John was twisting like an eel trying to get free but Brady's hands were too much of a match for him.

Myra pulled John's trousers down to his ankles and started fondling his genitals.

Screams of agony broke the silence, which lay on the moor like poison, as Brady raped him.

Grinning, Brady took hold of the dagger. It lay cold in his hands. It was short but so sharp even the most gentle of touches would slice the skin like slicing through butter.

Still lying on top of him, he lifted John's head, sneered, and slashed his throat.

"Give me his shoe," he screeched to Myra.

She tugged a shoe off of John's foot and gave it to Brady.

Brady removed the lace and tied it tightly round the boy's neck.

She stood there watching and hissing.

The silence returned to the moor. The fog wrapped itself around John's body like a cloak of death.

The eyes that were once sparkling were now vacant and staring. His mouth which smiled in a cheeky grin was now stiff and wide open. His arms lay lifelessly at his side. His legs twisted up to his chest. Somebody that was so much alive had

just been snuffed out like a candle.

Brady quickly dug the grave and rolled John's body into it. He took the whiskey bottle and said, "Here's to John."

Swigging the whiskey and spilling more than he drank, he raised his fist to the sky and shouted to God, "Take that you bastard. This place belongs to me. This is my sacred ground." He tossed the empty bottle onto the moor.

Turning to Myra he said, "I am supreme. I am my own god. I was created this way. You and I are one! All those beneath us have to be put down. Children should be kept on a leash like dogs."

"Come on," she said. "Let's go home."

"We haven't finished yet," Brady said. "There's one more thing we have to do."

"What's that?" she asked.

"You're going to spread your legs and I'm going to fuck you. While I'm fucking you I will smear the blood I have on my hands all over your body. This is my sacrifice to the Devil."

They arrived home very late. They had previously lined the inside of the car with plastic sheeting to save them the immaculate cleaning. However, they still burned the clothes they had been wearing.

"We're going to keep trophies from our hunting expeditions. But I'm burning this one," he said, as he threw the shoe he had taken from John into the fire. "We'll go up to the moor at the weekends and take photos of the graves and make sure nothing has been disturbed."

"I feel as if I have reached the point of no return," Myra said.

"It's good that you've admitted that," he said. "What is done is done. There's no going back. We are more bound together now the second murder is over."

The couple had become hunters. Their prey was innocent youngsters.

They couldn't quench their thirst for blood and continued their hunt for victims.

Their hunting season was whenever it took their fancy and their next victim was going to be another twelve year old boy.

The days were getting longer. June was moving on toward high summer. Flies were buzzing all around. The tarmacked roads were melting.

Myra and Ian had spent the afternoon at Belle Vue Zoo in Longsight, Manchester.

Brady had said he was an animal and wanted to spend time with the animals.

The heat pushed in on her and the sweat rolled down her forehead washing the mascara into her eyes. They both thought they were going to shrivel in the heat. Brady's shirt was wet from the sweat trickling down his back.

Keith Bennett had celebrated his birthday four days previously and was on his way to see his grandmother who lived in Longsight.

Every Tuesday he would spend the night at his gran's house. This Tuesday wasn't going to be any different for him, so he thought.

His grandmother's house was only a mile away from where he lived so he walked there by himself.

"Now go straight to your gran's Keith," his mum said, as she was watching him cross Stockport Road. "If I win at bingo tonight, I'll treat you tomorrow."

Like hunters waiting for their prey, they spotted him. They watched him for a while.

His clothes looked at least a size too small, only exaggerating his skinniness.

Myra pounced.

"Hello," she said. "You couldn't help me put some boxes in my car over there could you?"

"I'm on my way to my gran's," he replied.

"It won't take long," she said. "I can take you to your gran's if you help me."

"Okay," he said and went with her to the car.

"I've put the boxes in the back," Brady said,

"Oh," she said. "I just asked this young lad to help me."

"That's okay," Keith said.

"Well never mind," she said. "I'll give you a lift to your gran's anyway."

Keith, like another lamb going to slaughter, got into the car.

"Are you in much of a hurry?" she asked.

"Why?" he asked.

"I lost an expensive glove on the moor and I need some help to find it," she said. "It's a lovely afternoon. Could you help me look for it?"

"If I come with you will you take me to my gran's after?" he asked.

"Why of course," she replied, contorting her lips into an awkward, toothy smile.

"Okay then," he said.

They got to the moor and led Keith to his fate.

They were out of sight of the car which was parked in the layby.

Myra was holding Keith's hand and Brady went off in another direction.

They had walked for about two minutes when she turned to Keith and said, "I think it was here where I lost my glove," pointing down to the ground.

"I can't see very well without my glasses," he said. "I left them at home. Let me take a look."

He stooped down to look for the glove.

Brady came up from behind with the shovel he had hidden nearby.

He swiped it across the back of Keith's head.

Keith's eyesight became more blurry. His arms were desperately trying to reach out for something to grab hold of to save him from this horrible fate. He started feeling weak and crashed to the ground. He couldn't fight it any longer.

Brady stood over him with his legs apart while Myra pulled Keith's shorts down.

She touched and fondled his body while Brady prepared to penetrate him.

He took a piece of string and tied it round Keith's neck.

As he was raping the boy he pulled harder and harder on it until he heard Keith's last gasping breath.

Exhausted, he lifted himself up slowly and looked down at what now looked like a ghoulish puppet.

They dumped the body, like a rag doll, into the waiting grave.

Brady walked away brushing the loose peat from his jeans.

Myra followed behind adjusting the straps on her smart, leather handbag.

CHAPTER NINE

Myra, her gran, and Brady were having Christmas dinner in their new home. They had moved to a new housing estate in Hattersley because the houses in Gorton had been declared slums and were being demolished.

The Queen's speech on television was just coming to an end.

"All of us who have been blessed with young families know from long experience that when one's house is at its noisiest, there is often less cause for anxiety. The creaking of a ship in a heavy sea is music in the ears of the captain on the bridge. In fact little is static and without movement there can be no progress.

Some speak today as though the age of adventure and initiative is past. On the contrary, never have the challenges been greater or more urgent. The fight against poverty, malnutrition and ignorance is harder than ever, and we must do all in our power to see that science is directed towards solving these problems.

I would like to say one more word to the young people of the Commonwealth. Upon you rests our hope for the future. You young people are needed; there is a great task ahead of you - the building of a new world.

You have brains and courage, imagination and humanity; direct them to the things that have to be achieved in this century, if mankind is to live together in happiness and prosperity.

God bless you and a very, very happy Christmas to you all."

"Arrogant bitch," Brady said. "Another cunt being kept by the country."

"Don't use language like that in front of gran," Myra said.

"Well it's true what I'm saying," he said. "I can't stand the morons."

"By the way, I'm taking gran to some relatives early tomorrow," she said. "She's staying with them overnight. Do you want to come?"

"No," he replied. "I've got other plans."

Early the next day she took her gran to the relative's house.

"I'll come and pick you up tomorrow," she said.

"No," her gran said. "I want to come back tonight."

"You can't," Myra said.

"Why not?" she asked.

"Because me and Ian are going out and I won't have time," she replied.

While she was away Brady had arranged their bedroom.

He had placed a camera on top of the dressing table and positioned spotlights on top of the wardrobe. He had put the tape recorder Myra had bought him as a birthday present under the bed and placed a record player on the dressing table.

When Myra returned he showed her what he had done.

"What's all this in aid of?" she asked.

"It's been six months since we did our last murder and it's time to do another," he replied. "This time I want to take photos and record it. Your gran's out of the way so we have the opportunity to do it here. We can take the body up to the moor once it's over and done with. I want a little girl this time."

"Here's some pocket money," said Lesley Ann's mother. "You and your brothers can go to the fair this afternoon."

The snow had fallen like confetti onto the streets. The cold wind whispered in

their ears but they were wrapped up warm and were happy.

They were thrilled just walking towards the fairground. The fair wouldn't be visible until they turned the final corner but their expectations were building to a climax. Sounds of the fairground were already beginning to float through the air.

They hadn't been there too long when her brothers said, "We've spent all our money Lesley so we're going back home."

"I've still got sixpence left," she said. "I'm going to stay a little bit longer. I'll see you later."

"Well, remember you have to be back home by eight or you'll get a good hiding from mam," one of her brothers said.

Myra and Brady were considering where to look for a child.

"There's a fair in Ancoats this week," said Brady. "I'm sure we'll find someone there."

"Don't you think that's taking a risk?" Myra asked.

He was getting so confident that they would never be found out.

"There'll be hundreds of people at the fairground," he replied. "Nobody's going to notice one go missing."

Off they went on their hunting spree again.

Lesley Ann was happy standing watching the Waltzers spinning around and tapping her feet to the loud music booming in her ears. She was like Alice in Wonderland thinking about what to do with her sixpenny bit. Her face was angelic. The cold wind had given her cheeks a rosy hue.

Brady's eyes zoomed in on her like an eagle.

Standing there was a little girl on her own. Her size told him she would be about ten years old.

"She's the one," he said nudging Myra.

When they got close enough to her, Myra deliberately let some of the shopping she was carrying fall near the little girl.

Lesley Ann turned around.

"Oh dear," said Myra. "I hope I haven't broken the eggs. Could you help me carry some of these packages to my car and then to my house?"

she asked. "I'll give you some money and you can come back here and spend it."

"Yes," Lesley Ann replied.

Brady went into the house first while Myra and Lesley Ann were getting the shopping out of the car. He went straight upstairs to the bedroom and waited.

Myra took Lesley Ann into the house and locked the door behind her.

Going up the stairs she called, "Can you bring the shopping up here? Then I'll take you back to the fair."

Lesley Ann followed.

As soon as she got into the bedroom Brady grabbed her and started undressing her.

Her eyes wide with horror, her mouth rigid and open, her fists clenched and her nails digging deeply into the palms of her hands, Lesley screamed.

Brady turned on the tape.

"This is track four," he said. "Get out of the fucking road and get into the basket."

He blew into the microphone attached to the tape recorder then left the room

banging the door behind him

Myra went over to Lesley Ann.

"Don't. Mum – Ah," she screamed.

"Come on," said Myra. "Shut up!"

"Oh, please," said Lesley Ann pleading. "Oh. Help."

"Sh. Sh," said Myra. "Shut up. Shut up."

"Oh. Oh. Oh," Lesley said crying.

"Keep still and you'll be all right," whispered Myra. "Go on."

Brady ran quickly back upstairs and into the bedroom.

Lesley Ann was still crying.

"Here," he whispered to her.

"Hush, hush," Myra said to Lesley Ann, giving her a scarf. "Go on. You are all right. Hush, hush. Put it in your mouth and shift that hand."

Lesley Ann continued crying.

"Put it in your mouth and keep it in and you'll be all right," she said. "Put it in, stop it. If you don't—sh…"

Lesley Ann was now whimpering.

"Put it in," Brady said.

"Put it in," Myra said quickly.

"Put it in. Keep it in. Stop it now. Stop it now," said Brady.

"I'm only doing this and you'll be all right," said Myra. "Put it in your mouth. Put it in - in. Will you stop it? Stop it."

Lesley Ann continued whimpering.

"Shut up!" screamed Myra.

"Quick," said Brady. "Put it in now."

Lesley Ann retched.

"Just put it in now, love. Put it in now," said Brady.

Lesley Ann retched again. "What's this in for?" she asked.

"Put it in," Brady said.

"Can I just tell you summat? I must tell you summat," Lesley Ann said. "Please, take your hands off me a minute, please, please—Mummy—please. I can't tell you."

She started grunting then quickly said, "I can't tell you, I can't breathe. Oh. I can't—Dad-Will you take your hands off me?"

"No," Brady whispered. "No. Tell me."

"Please God," said Lesley Ann.

"Tell me," said Brady.

"I can't while you've got your hands on me," she said.

"Why don't you keep it in?" Brady asked.

"Why? What are you going to do with me?" she asked. "

"I want some photographs, that's all," said Brady. "Put it in."

"Don't undress me, will you?" she asked.

"That's right, don't—," said Myra.

"It hurts me. I want to see Mummy, honest to God," Lesley Ann said.

"Put it in," Brady said.

"I'll swear on the Bible," said Lesley Ann.

"Put it in, and hurry up now," said Brady. "The quicker you do this, the quicker you'll get home."

"I've got to go, because I'm going out with my Mamma," she said. "Leave me, please. Help me, will you?"

"Put it in your mouth and you'll be all right," Brady replied.

"Will you let me go when this is out?" she asked.

"Yes," Brady replied. "The longer it takes you to do this, the longer it takes you to get home."

"What are you going to do with me first?" she asked.

"I'm going to take some photographs," he replied. "Put it in your mouth."

"What for?" she asked.

"Put it in your mouth," he said. "Right in."

"I'm not going to do owt," she said.

"Put it in," he said. "If you don't keep that hand down, I'll slit your neck. Put it in."

"Won't you let me go? Please," she begged.

"No, no. Put it in, stop talking," he replied. "What's your name?"

"Lesley," she replied.

"Lesley what?" he asked.

"Ann," she replied.

"What's your second name?" he asked.

"Westford," she replied. "Westford."

"Westford?" he asked.

"I have to get home before 8 o'clock," she replied. "I got to get ...., or I'll get killed if I don't. Honest to God."

"Yes," he said.

Myra left the room quickly and went downstairs.

Brady took photos of Lesley Ann.

Myra came back upstairs and into the bedroom.

"What is it?" he asked.

"I've left the light on," she replied.

"You have?" he asked.

Lesley Ann started crying. "It hurts me neck," she said.

"Hush, put it in your mouth and you'll be all right," he said.

"Now listen, shurrup crying," Myra said.

"It hurts on me," Lesley Ann said crying.

"Hush! Shut up. Now, put it in," said Myra. "Pull that hand away and don't dally and just keep your mouth shut, please. Wait a bit; I'll put this on again. Do you get me?"

"No," replied Lesley Ann, whining.

"Sh. Hush. Put that in your mouth," said Myra. "And again, packed more solid."

"I want to go home," said Lesley. "Honest to God. I'll be killed if I don't get home before eight o'clock."

"No, it's all right," said Myra.

"Eh!" said Brady.

Placing a gramophone record onto the record player, Myra placed the needle down on the record. A fine crackling sound followed as the needle touched it. The music began.

Brady got on top of Lesley Ann. Putting his hands around her neck he squeezed tightly. She was terrified and choking. Her eyes became round and her lips parted. Her legs shuddered. His climax was almost there. His grip got tighter as his pleasure increased. Her eyes closed and her body went limp. That's what he wanted. He ejaculated immediately. He dismounted her and left Myra to wash the

lifeless body ready for disposal on the moor the following day whilst he went to take a bath.

The last thing little Lesley Ann heard, as her life was being squeezed from her, was The Little Drummer Boy Christmas song.

A far cry from the loud music she had been happily tapping her feet to a few hours before at the fairground.

Myra had to pick her gran up that day so they had to go to the moor early and dispose of the body.

All that could be seen in front of them was a carpet of white, rolling for miles and covering the moor.

Brady recovered the shovel he had hidden, which had now been buried by snow, and they buried the naked body of Lesley Ann, with her clothes at her feet, in a shallow grave.

They had claimed their fourth trophy.

CHAPTER TEN

Myra's sister, Maureen, got married to David Smith in August 1964, two months after Brady and Myra had murdered Keith Bennett.

She was seven months pregnant. She had a baby daughter named Angela. The baby died six months later, four months after they had murdered Lesley Ann Downey.

Maureen and David were psychologically affected by the death of their child and this had started to affect their marriage.

David lost his job and had to try to maintain both of them on his dole money.

They had a flat close by to where Myra lived with her gran and Brady.

They owed rent and the council was going to evict them.

Maureen was pregnant again and very worried about the eviction notice.

"The council have given us one more week to pay the rent we owe or we're out," she said to David. "Where are we going to get the money from?"

"I'll go and talk to Ian," he replied. "I'll ask him if he can lend us some money. I'll tell Myra you want to see her so I can talk to him alone."

He went to Myra's house.

"Hello David. How are you feeling?" she asked.

"I'm okay under the circumstances," he replied.

"And how's our Maureen?" she asked.

"That's why I'm here," he replied. "She'd like to talk to you. She's very depressed."

Grabbing her coat she said, "I'll go round right away. Ian's in the front room. Go and have a beer with him."

She had never liked David and had noticed that he was becoming over friendly with Brady. She thought he was coming between them.

"Hey Dave," Brady said. "What's up?"

"Maureen's feeling under the weather," he replied. "She wants to see Myra."

Well let's drink some wine and cheer you up," Brady said.

David didn't want to ask Brady outright to lend him money. He would chat with him about this and that and then raise the topic.

"The police haven't found Pauline Reade yet, have they?" he asked.

"Who?" Brady asked.

"Pauline," he replied. You know the girl who lived a door away from me when we were living in Gorton."

"Oh her," he said.

"Did you know she was my girlfriend before I met Maureen?" he asked.

"Myra did mention something," he replied.

"Just after she went missing," David said. "The police gave me hell. They thought I had something to do with it."

"The cops are fucking morons," Brady said. "They do fuck all."

"It's been almost two years since she disappeared," he said. "I think she's dead."

Brady made no comment and poured them another drink.

"Since she disappeared," David continued. "Three kids have also gone missing."

"What?" asked Brady.

"I said three other kids have gone missing," he replied.

"I blame the parents," said Brady. "They shouldn't let kids go out on their own."

"The cops think these disappearances are linked," he said.

"How's that then?" he asked.

"Ashton, Longsight and Ancoats," he replied. "It's a triangular area. Maybe the bloke who's done it lives in the triangle. He was probably living in Gorton before the place was knocked down."

"What makes you think a bloke did it," he asked.

"Women don't do those kinds of things," he replied.

"Well I knew Pauline pretty well," David said. "She'd never go off with someone she didn't know."

"We might never find that out," Brady said.

"Remember when we went onto the moor for Myra's birthday?" he asked. "I told you that I had killed a guy in Glasgow."

"Yes I remember," he replied. "I find it very hard to believe."

"I've killed others," he said.

"You don't half talk some crap," said David.

"You don't believe me, do you?" he asked. "You stood on one of the graves."

"Bollocks," said David drinking more wine.

"If you think it's bollocks then think it," he said.

David could see that Brady was relaxed with the effect of the wine and thought that now would be a good time to change the subject and ask for the money.

"Hey Ian," he said. "I also remember that day on the moor when you said you wanted to do a bank job."

"What about it?" he asked.

"You asked me to observe the bank on Hyde Road and take notes. I did," he replied. "When I gave them to you, you showed no interest and chucked them away."

"That's because I had other plans," he said.

"Just wishful thinking then?" he asked. "You're all fucking talk."

"Why are you suddenly interested in a bank job?" he asked. "When I mentioned it up there you were almost shitting yourself with fright."

"Well, if I don't raise some cash Maureen will leave me," he replied. "We owe the council rent and I need this money by next Saturday or they'll kick us out."

"I might have the solution for you," he said.

"What would that be?" he asked.

"We could go to the Rembrandt bar," he replied. "The one where the Nancy boys hang out and get the money from a queer. You know, a business man. We could bring him back here and threaten to beat him up if he didn't give us the dough. I think he'd hand it over rather than have to tell his wife why he got beat up."

"Wouldn't he go to the police?" he asked.

"Would you go to the police if you were queer?" Brady replied.

"I don't suppose I would," David replied. "Sounds like a good idea. When?"

Pointing to two suitcases in the corner Brady replied, "I want you to take these to the left luggage office at the railway station."

"What's inside?" he asked.

"None of your business," he replied. "Just do it. Now fuck off and wait till I call

for you."

David took the cases and left.

Brady knew he was now in control of David and had him in the palm of his hands. He'd been testing him just as he had done with Myra in the early days. However, he would find out that this test was going to backfire on him sooner

rather than later.

Halloween was just around the corner. The days were getting shorter. The streetlamps on both sides of Wardle Brook Avenue flickered on. Their artificial light illuminating the fallen leaves on the pavement.

"Remember when I told you I was having it off with another bloke?" Brady asked Myra.

"Vaguely," she replied. "To be honest with you I wasn't taking much notice."

Well I've been planning this for ages," he said.

"Planning what?" she asked.

"Another murder," he replied. "Tonight's the night. I've got a date with him. You can drive me to Central Station and I'll pick him up and bring him back here and kill the bastard."

"But gran's upstairs," she said.

"That's no problem," he said. "It'll be over and done with in no time. We're going to involve Dave in this one. If anything goes wrong we can blame him. His word against yours and mine."

She drove him to the station and waited in the car while Brady went to meet Eddie.

In the daytime the station was a seething mass of commuters but now there was space.

Eddie was leaning against the platform ticket machine.

Brady whistled and he turned around.

"Fancy coming back to my place for a drink?" Brady asked.

"Aren't we going to the Rembrandt?" Eddie asked.

"Change of plan," Brady replied. "I thought we could have a cosy night together with a few glasses of wine."

He nudged Eddie and said, "Then later we can have a bit of you know what."

Raising his eyebrows and pressing his lips together, "Mm, sounds good to me," Eddie said.

"Come on then," he said. "We don't have to catch the bus. My sister's waiting for us in her car."

Brady reappeared accompanied by Eddie.

When Myra saw how the young man was walking she could tell he was effeminate.

After Brady had introduced him to her, Eddie's voice proved he was.

"This is my sister," Brady said.

"Ooh," Eddie squealed, "Nice to meet you chuck."

She drove them back home and the three of them sat drinking wine.

Gran had gone to bed.

"Can you go round and get Dave?" Brady asked Myra. "I've got some miniature bottles of wine I promised him."

Maureen and David had gone to bed early that night and a loud knocking on the
door woke them up.

"I wonder who that could be." Maureen said. "Go and see who it is."

David went downstairs and opened the front door.

He shouted to Maureen, "It's your Myra."

She came downstairs with rollers in her hair and still wearing her nightie.

"Can I come in?" Myra asked.

"Sure," replied Maureen. "What brings you here at this time of night?"

"I know you're seeing mam tomorrow and I want you to give her a message," she replied.

"What message?" she asked.

"Tell her I'll pop round tomorrow so she can touch my roots up," she replied. "I would have come round earlier but I got distracted."

"Right I'll tell her," she said.

"Would you walk me back home Dave?" Myra asked. "It's darker than I thought and I don't want to walk back on my own."

"Why didn't Ian come with you?" he asked.

"He's doing some business with a bloke," she replied.

Okay," he said. "Come on let's go."

"Don't be long," Maureen said.

"I won't," he said, and left the house with Myra.

When they got to Myra's house she turned to him and said, "Wait out here. When you see the lights upstairs flash, knock on the door."

She went inside.

David saw the signal and knocked on the door.

Brady answered the door.

"Have you come for those miniature wine bottles?" he asked. "You'd better come in."

Brady took David into the kitchen.

"What the fuck are you talking about?" he asked. "What miniature bottles of wine?"

"You want the money for the rent, don't you?" Brady asked. "I picked up a business man and he's in the front room. Now fucking wait here."

David almost jumped out of his skin when he heard a scream. It made the hair on the back of his neck stand up. It was the loudest most piercing scream he had ever heard. It sounded like a woman screaming in terror.

"Dave, help him," shouted Myra.

He ran into the front room and froze.

A young man was lying with his head and shoulders on the couch and his legs on the floor.

Brady was striking him on the left side of his head with the flat of an axe.

He screamed again and Brady said, "Shut up you fucking bastard. You fucking queer."

He swung the axe again but missed and hit himself on the ankle with it.

"Cunt," Brady screamed and bought the axe down again on Eddie.

Eddie slumped to the floor, choking on his own blood.

Myra stood watching with her arms folded and tittering.

Brady snatched at a table lamp and throttled Eddie with the cable. Everything went silent.

"Myra," gran's voice shouted from upstairs. "What the bloody hell's going on down there?"

"It's all right gran," she shouted back. "I dropped the tape recorder on my foot."

She went into the kitchen to make some tea.

"Feel the weight of this," Brady said, handing the axe to David.

"I don't want to touch it," he said.

Brady put the axe down. The sweat trickled down his face. It beaded on his forehead and dripped from his chin.

He wiped the sweat away. A grin spread over his face, wide and open, showing his smoke stained teeth.

In that instant David's skin became greyed. His mouth hung with lips slightly parted and his eyes were as wide as they could stretch. He had nothing to say but empty words.

Brady headed for the kitchen.

David's bowels suddenly churned. He followed Brady into the kitchen fighting the need to vomit.

"Did you see the look on his face when the axe came down?" Brady asked, chuckling and drinking his tea.

"I saw the blow register in his eyes," Myra said, hardly capable of breathing for laughing. "The fucking idiot."

"That one was the messiest yet," Brady said. "Now that one's over we'll have to think about doing the next."

A cold chill ran down David's spine.

"Would you like a chocolate biscuit?" Myra asked.

"No thanks," he replied.

"Have a fag then," she said.

He took a cigarette from her hoping his hand wouldn't shake. He lit it and inhaled deeply.

"Well we'd better finish this tea and start cleaning up the mess," Brady said.

The body had slumped to the floor like a carcass at the butchers. The eyes remained open, staring blankly at the ceiling. There were bits of bone and hair on the floor. Some brain matter had exploded from the side of the skull and splattered on the wall.

The room smelled like an abattoir.

"We'll have to move the body first," said Brady. "Myra go and get the plastic sheets out of the car."

She fetched the sheets and they wrapped Eddie's body in them.

"I've hurt my fucking ankle hitting the bastard with the axe," Brady said. "I can't lift him myself. You'll have to help me carry him upstairs Dave. Make sure no blood drips on the stairs."

They took the body up to the spare room.

David followed Brady's instructions on making sure that no trace of anything was left in the front room as he helped them clean up. He knew if he didn't go along with them he would be the next.

While they were cleaning up Myra was picking up the bits of bone and hair off the floor without seeming to have any problem with it.

"This is a dream! A nightmare," he thought, shaking his head. "It's not real. How could it be?"

He was hoping that everything would go away and he would wake up in his bed. But it wasn't a nightmare. It was for real.

It was getting late. He'd told Maureen he wouldn't be gone long. He thought he'd gone round to Myra's house to get money to pay the rent. The rent arrears were now the last thing on his mind.

"Look Myra," he said stuttering. "I'll have to go. I'll come back early in the morning and help you get rid of the body."

"Don't you want to stay and have some supper with us?" she asked, smiling without a care in the world.

He shook his head trying hard not to show his fear.

"Okay then," she said. "Tell Mo I'll see her at mum's house tomorrow. Oh, and don't forget to bring Angela's pram with you. We don't want the neighbours seeing us carrying a dead body out of the house."

He walked away casually. As soon as he was out of sight of the house he ran back home for his life.

Maureen was fast asleep.

He shook her hard to get her to wake up.

When she turned at last to face him her eyes were narrowed, rigid, cold, and hard. Her fists began to clench showing the whites of her knuckles. Then she exploded.

"You said you wouldn't be gone long," she said. "Look at the fucking time. You know we have to pay the rent on Saturday or we're out but you prefer to get as pissed as a fart with fucking Ian!"

"I'm not drunk," he said. "Ian's just beaten a young kid to death with an axe right in front of my eyes."

"What?" she asked, "Now I know you're drunk."

"I told you I'm not fucking drunk," he said. "And Myra was in on it. They'd planned it together and they're planning more. She's evil. You know what Maureen, Brady sleeps with the Devil. The Devil is your sister."

She backed away. Nothing about this was making sense.

"I can't believe what I'm hearing," she said.

"I swear to God it's true," he said. "What I just witnessed was my worst nightmare. They want me to go round in the morning with Angela's pram to help get rid of the body."

"Then we have to go to the police," she said. "Now."

Finally, Brady and Myra's killing spree had come to an end.

CHAPTER ELEVEN

C ould it be that notorious child killer Myra Hindley, who allegedly had links to Jimmy Savile, is not actually dead?

On the 15th November 2002 Moors Murderer Myra Hindley, 60, was said to have died in the West Suffolk Hospital at Bury St. Edmunds after a chest infection which hospitalized her on November 12th – following a suspected heart attack two weeks previously. She was said to have received the last rites from a Catholic priest in her bed at 4.55 am after a disturbed night in her isolated solitary ward.

On 18th November Greater Suffolk coroner Peter Dean was told by Home Office pathologist Dr Michael Heath, who carried out the post mortem examination at West Suffolk hospital, that Hindley died of bronchial pneumonia due to heart problems.

She suffered from high blood pressure and poor blood supply to the heart, resulting in blocked coronary arteries, he said.

In surprising haste she was cremated on 20th November 2002 although no family members attended. She was reported to be cremated following the service at the crematorium.

The inquest into Hindley's death was opened and adjourned at Highpoint Prison near Bury St Edmunds, Suffolk and a jury hearing was scheduled to take place at a later date. It opened on January 23rd 2003 at medium security Highpoint prison, Suffolk. It was disclosed that in her final months Hindley, 60, had been prescribed a range of 24 drugs for a range of problems including angina, asthma, bronchitis, osteoporosis, osteoarthritis and raised cholesterol including temazapam for insomnia.

In a unique arrangement for such an inquest there were no protesters, friends or relatives at the resumed inquest because of the intense media interest in Hindley therefore it was convened in a Highpoint building used for the training of officers at the desolate prison.

The jury of eight women and three men took 48 minutes to reach the unanimous decision that Hindley, died of natural causes: bronchial pneumonia, brought on by hypertension and coronary heart disease.

Her medical records were filed under a false name: Christine Charlton.

Graham Cook, a fingerprint expert with Suffolk Police, said that he had compared Hindley's prints with those on the National Fingerprint Archive, which had been taken in October 1965 in Cheshire, and was able to confirm the identity of the dead woman beyond doubt.

Hospital staff, some of whom attended the inquest, redecorated Hindley's room after she died.

Her ashes are said to have been be scattered at an undisclosed location. Her death certificate has never been published – but presumably exists in official records somewhere.

A curious tale in which the only direct evidence is from a small circle of employees of the Home Office.

A plausible tale which a reliable, honest, respectable and well informed contact assures us forms the basis of an elaborate agreement for Myra Hindley's release

from custody, very much alive, after she had served double the sentence usually served by convicted murderers with good records of behaviour. A subject which has been very recently widely discussed by social workers at a senior level in a

certain area of the UK.

We then find this shocking eye-witness report:

A primary school nurse was driving through a country lane about six weeks after Myra Hindley was supposedly pronounced dead. It was night time and the nurse's car was suddenly hit in the back by another vehicle.

The woman driver who hit her got out of her car and came to talk to the nurse. The nurse looked carefully, recognised the woman as Myra Hindley and said, "Oh my God you're Myra Hindley."

The woman burst into tears and replied, "You can't say that. You can't say that," and drove off hurriedly.

The nurse however, noted the registration number of the car and upon returning home called the police. She recounted what had happened, telling them that it was "Myra Hindley" at the wheel of the other car.

The police visited the nurse the following day but rather than assist her with noting an accident, they scared and intimidated her. They asked her to withdraw the accident claim and report, and suggested instead that the incident had "never happened".

The primary school nurse was just a normal, law-abiding person and by now she was very scared although still certain of her facts – that even though Myra Hindley was believed by the world to be dead – it had been her driving the car that had hit her.

Regardless of her story, the police continued to intimidate the nurse and she was frightened into taking any further action.

However, unknown to the police, the nurse had reported the incident to a friend of the family who had in turn passed it on to a school friend who was a local journalist.

The journalist took the story to a major tabloid paper who was at first very interested but the following day told his fellow journalist that the story of Hindley being alive "had to be buried."

Despite this, within a day or so, orders from "the top" were given to publish a story on how the "ashes of Myra Hindley had been found."

That story made all the papers in February 2003 and threw many off the scent. Now, to all intent and purposes, Hindley was proven to be dead because her ashes had been found on the very Moors where children had been killed.

What is interesting is that the car incident happened six miles away from the residence of the priest that converted Myra Hindley to Catholicism and who later committed burial rites on her.

What is further interesting is the location of a convent very close by. Is Myra Hindley in that convent living a clandestine life away from society?

Not satisfied with the tale of ashes being discovered and believing the story of the nurse, the journalist called Lord Longford's son and informed him that the ashes of Myra Hindley had been found. The journalist taped the conversation. The words from Longford's son echoed in the journalists ears:

"If you believe that, you'll believe anything".

Yet as the years rolled by, with the advent of the United Kingdom immersed into a European Union, the suddenly realisation of EU human rights law became apparent after Tony Blair signed it into law. Myra Hindley was entitled to know her release date from prison, and home secretaries were not allowed to determine sentence. That was ruled exclusively the right of judges. New Labour knew they couldn't risk seeing Hindley walk free from prison.

The backlash at the ballot box could spell disaster for the new labour project, and so I believe a plot was hatched to free Myra Hindley under a joint consensus of government, the prison and probation service and Hindley herself. The government would, in return for her silence paint an elaborate hoax and dupe the British people. But in doing, make one fundamental error which would lead to the whole plan collapsing.

With a witness protection programme already in place to protect supergrasses and terrorists who decide to turn on their own people, the government created a cynical plan. Myra Hindley would be offered plastic surgery, a new

identity and relocated to pastures new: possibly overseas in another European country.

For a year or two Myra Hindley was ferried back and forth to hospital under the pretext she had heart problems, although, any sign of this condition evaporates when we examine press photos of Myra at Cookham Wood prison. After her hospital visits, Myra can quite easily be seen puffing away on packs of cigarettes.

Not the image of someone with heart problems. Most people might expect Myra to have been towing an oxygen bottle, not chain smoking. Once her new identity and paperwork were complete, with new documents and a new history, national insurance number and passport, Myra's faked death took place. To this day, no doctor or nurse has come forward to discuss Myra Hindley's final hours, even though the tabloid press would offer them a blank cheque for their story. Normally, hospital administrators can't be kept away from the cameras with a big stick. But not on this occasion With Myra receiving her new face, hair style and identity, the prison service announced a short statement to the press: "Myra Hindley died peacefully in her sleep."

With her death revealed to the waiting press and wider world, all that was needed was a funeral. This was hurriedly arranged. With television reporters and tabloid journalists huddled round the gates of the crematorium, Myra's coffin was whisked in. But was she in the coffin?

The fatal flaw in the home office plan is, Myra Hindley was, is, a devout Catholic. And here lies the error: you don't cremate Catholics. To a Catholic, cremation is a cardinal sin and prohibits them from passing through the gates of heaven. Hindley would have left explicit instructions for her funeral, and these would have been followed to the letter by a politically correct prison service. Does anyone believe in this day and age, the prison service would countenance the sanctity of the church, the individual's religion? Of course not. Hindley never died. She was released by a new labour government frightened the European court of human rights would do the job for them, cost them votes at the ballot box and give the opposition parties a big stick to beat them with. That's how it works in Britain.

BEWARE

If you see a little old lady walking with a dog and offering young children sweets

take heed.

It could be the DEVIL herself!!

The End

THE COST

I an Brady has cost taxpayers £14MILLION since he was jailed nearly 50 years ago

* High security psychiatric unit alone has cost £7.6m for Brady's 28-year stay.

* Keeping murderer in mental health unit costs eight times more than prison.

* His various legal challenges have cost £2.75million in legal and admin fees.

* His 14-year hunger strike has added around £3million to the bill.

Expensive: It is costing at least £273,000 per year to keep murderer Ian Brady in a high security psychiatric unit.

Taxpayers have forked out more than £14million on Ian Brady since he was convicted nearly 50 years ago.

The Moors murderer, who tortured and killed five children with his then girlfriend Myra Hindley, has racked up the costs of his keep by staging a 14-year hunger strike and a series of failed legal challenges - for which he has

relied on legal aid.

Brady, now 75, spent 19 years as a Category A prisoner after his conviction in 1966, spending time in Wormwood Scrubs, Durham, Parkhurst and Gartree prisons at a cost of at least £750,000 - according to recent figures.

In 1985 he was transferred to a high security psychiatric unit at Park Lane Special Hospital - now Ashworth – in Merseyside, after being diagnosed as psychotic.

The cost of keeping him there for 28 years has been around £7.6million, according to the latest figures which put the cost of keeping a person in a high security unit at an average of £749 a day - or £273,000 a year.

It is almost eight times more expensive holding Brady in the mental health unit than in a prison, which would cost around £40,000 per year.

The difference is largely made up from the salaries of the huge numbers of specialist staff needed to maintain security and care for the high risk patients at Ashworth, including 11 consultants and 649 nursing staff along with psychiatrists and psychologists, social workers, occupational therapists, teachers, physical health care staff, chaplains, cooks, cleaners and security staff.

But the price of keeping the murderer alive has been dramatically increased since 1999 when he went on hunger strike in protest at being moved to a ward for people with severe personality disorders.

It is thought force-feeding Brady through a tube has cost around £3million, including around £2.3million for the salaries of specialist mental health nurses who have to watch him around the clock.

TAXPAYERS' BILL FOR BRADY
Category A prison for 19 years - £760,000
High security psychiatric unit for 28 years - £7.6million
Force feeding for 14 years - £3million
Legal aid - £500,000
Mental health tribunal - £250,000
Whitehall administrative and legal costs - £2million
TOTAL = £14.11million

And the killer has also launched a series of expensive legal challenges against the hospital trust, believed to have cost around £500,000 in legal aid.

His current mental health tribunal - where he is appealing to be ruled sane so he can be transferred to a normal prison and be allowed to starve himself to death - is

reportedly costing the taxpayer around £250,000.

And the knock-on effect of his string of legal actions against the government means Whitehall staff have spent around £2million in time and legal costs battling with the killer, The Sun reported.

The total cost to the taxpayer of Brady's 57 years in captivity is around £14.1million.

Relatives of the five children murdered by Brady and Myra Hindley in the 1960s have said the money would be better spent tracing the remains of Keith Bennett, the location of which Brady refuses to reveal.

Matthew Sinclair, chief executive of the 'Taxpayers' Alliance, told Mail Online: 'Universal access to justice is important, however the system must be administered with reasonable and proportionate costs.

'It's deeply unfair that Brady has been allowed to exploit taxpayers even further through all the recent legal wrangling over his incarceration.

'This is another blow to the victims' families and also to taxpayers who already bear the burden to keep the unrepentant killer locked up.'

The Ministry of Justice declined to comment on the figures.

HOW THE MURDERS AFFECTED FAMILIES OF THE VICTIMS

J oan Reade, Pauline Reade's mother, was admitted to Springfield Mental Hospital in Manchester.

Five years after their son was murdered, Sheila and Patrick Kilbride divorced.

Ann West, mother of Lesley Ann Downey, died in 1999 from cancer of the liver. Since her daughter's death, she had campaigned to ensure that Hindley remained in prison, and doctors said that the stress had contributed to the severity of

her illness.

Winnie Johnson, mother of Keith Bennett, continued to visit Saddleworth Moor, where it is believed that the body of her son is buried. She died in August 2012.

In 1980 Maureen suffered a brain haemorrhage; Hindley was granted permission to visit her sister in hospital, but she arrived an hour after Maureen's death.

Shortly before her death at the age of 70 Sheila Kilbride said: "If Hindley ever comes out of jail I'll kill her." It was a threat repeated by her son Danny, and Ann West, mother of Lesley Ann Downey.

Maureen managed to repair the relationship with her mother, and moved into a council property in Gorton. She divorced Smith in 1973, and married a lorry driver, Bill Scott, with whom she had a daughter.

She and her immediate family made regular visits to see Hindley, who reportedly adored her niece.

In 1972 David Smith was acquitted of the murder of his father, who had been suffering from an incurable cancer. Smith pleaded guilty to manslaughter and was sentenced to two days' detention. He remarried and moved to Lincolnshire with his three sons, and was exonerated of any participation in the Moors murders by Hindley's confession in 1987. He died in Ireland in 2012. David Smith said of the families of the victims:

To term me as a Moors murder case victim is wrong. No, that's the parents. They're the victims. It's them I bleed for. I'm a survivor. I survived. I am not a victim of it. I got through it. Lots of the parents are frozen in time. Their memories stopped in the sixties. They still see their missing children the same size. They never grew. They never got older. They never changed. They're the victims.

FINAL WORD

Between 1963 and 1965 Ian Brady and Myra Hindley went on a murder spree just for kicks. They were found guilty and sentenced to life imprisonment in May 1966.

They escaped the death penalty by a matter of months.

Five other children went missing in the Manchester area during that period and are still missing. Are those children also buried on Saddleworth moor?

Ian Brady is still alive and has spent just over 50 years locked away. He is currently in a high security psychiatric unit at Ashworth Hospital, Liverpool. He is still being maintained by the British tax payer.

Most of the members of his victims' families are no longer with us.

Myra Hindley is supposed to have died in 2002 after having spent 36 years in jail. But still there is doubt. Is she really dead? Or is she living under another identity?

Until Keith Bennett's body is found Brady and Hindley will have committed The Perfect Murder.

HARD TO BELIEVE?

This is a conversation, word for word, that the author had on Facebook, with a woman claiming to be the daughter of Myra Hindley.

8th March 2016.

Daughter: "Hi can I private message you? I think you will find this to your taste. I am the daughter of someone you are doing a book on."

Author: "Yes you can pm me. What book are you talking about? If you are talking about the book I'm writing: The Devil Knows, whose daughter are you and what would you like to tell me?"

Daughter: "Her name is beginning with M and H. I am looking to write a book of my own and can you please advise me on me how to go about doing it? Please do. Her name is Myra Hindley."

Author: "If you are the daughter of Myra Hindley who is your father? I have to admit you look a little like her though."

Daughter: "She gave me many men's names. I was not brought up by her I was brought up by another man. He is my father in my eyes."

Author: "The book I'm writing is about her relationship with Ian Brady. Could you give me any details? And how do you feel? And is she really dead?"

Daughter: "Yep some but not on here."

Author: "No of course not. You can email me if you like."

Daughter: "I would like to meet you beforehand."

Author: "I live in Mexico. How old was she then when you were born?"

Daughter: " Oh lol that's too far: I am in Glasgow but lived in Pimlico when she was taken to jail."

Author: "I remember the case. I was 17 at the time and living in the Midlands."

Daughter: "My dad was a caretaker there and he brought me to Glasgow when she went to prison."

Author: "The press never said anything about a daughter."

Daughter: "No I am supposed to be dead lol but am not. I just found out who I am 5 years ago."

Author: "And how do you feel knowing you are her daughter?"

Daughter: " I am now a gran."

Author: "That's nice to hear. How old were you when she went into prison?"

Daughter: "11."

Author: "Then you were born before she met Ian Brady?"

Daughter: "Let's just say her story and his is still going on to this day."

Author: "It will always go on. Maybe it will stop when he dies. And are you thinking about writing a book about her?

Daughter: "Don't believe what you read in the paper and see on TV."

Author: "I never do. Is there anything else you'd like to tell me about your mother?"

Daughter: "No I am keeping it for a book I would like to write. I just don't know how to go about it and getting started."

Author:Ok. "Well I am well into my book and hope it's published in a couple of weeks' time. If you are serious about writing the book and it is about her, people will find out who you are."

Daughter: "Some people already know who I am. Will I be able to buy your book in Glasgow?"

Author: "The book will be available on Amazon."

Daughter: "I will buy it."

Author: "I think you will find my book interesting and surprising."

Daughter: "My spelling is not too good as I was kept off school when she was drunk."

Author: "If you are, who you say you are, why won't you tell me things about your mom?"

Daughter: "Because I want it in my own book. Things other people don't know about her."

Author: "Sorry but I don't believe what you are saying."

Daughter: "That's ok. I am sorry you think that."

Author: "You said you were 11 when Myra went to jail. She would only have been 13 when she had you. You said she didn't bring you up and now you are telling me that you were kept off school because she was always drunk. You were born in 1962. Myra was jailed in 1966."

Daughter: "No she was raped by a man. I am the result of this and she was 15. I was brought up by my dad and she killed the caretaker in the 70s when we lived in Pimlico, London. My dad was the caretaker. And when she slit her wrists an agent went to hospital with her cos police were coming to take her away."

Author: "I'm sorry to hear that. It must be awful for you to have had to live with what she did to those kids."

Daughter: " Yes but I didn't know about that till 2 yearsago. She was not always bad. She was funny, and a good cook. The police gave her a wig to wear in court. She dyed her hair because her hair was black."

Author: "I don't wish to offend you but you are contradicting yourself. You said that Myra didn't bring you up. Now you are telling me she was funny and a good cook. You say that Myra was raped and you were the result and that she was 15 when you were born. Myra was born in 1942 so if she was 15 when you were born, you would have been born in 1957. You were born on Nov 4th 1962 according to the info on your Facebook profile. How could she have killed the caretaker in the 70's when she was jailed in 1966? You'll have to do better than that to convince me that you are Myra Hindley's daughter."

IAN BRADY DIED ON MAY 15th 2017 two months after this book was first published.

Don't miss out!

Visit the website below and you can sign up to receive emails whenever David J Cooper publishes a new book. There's no charge and no obligation.

https://books2read.com/r/B-A-CBBF-MZOP

BOOKS 2 READ

Connecting independent readers to independent writers.

Did you love *The Devil Knows*? Then you should read *Foul Play*[1] by David J Cooper!

Juan Carlos enjoys the Sunday afternoon before Easter by going with a friend to a nearby lake. In the early hours of the next morning he is found dead in his car. His family receive evidence proving that his death wasn't an accident. Why did the police say it was an accident when there was no sign of skid marks on the road surface? Why didn't the person who made the anonymous phone call reporting the accident wait at the scene till help arrived? Will his family face death threats if they continue investigating? Can they convince the corrupt Mexican legal system to arrest his killers? This story will make you think twice before visiting Mexico

Read more at davidjcooperauthorblog.wordpress.com.

---

1. https://books2read.com/u/4DZZlA

2. https://books2read.com/u/4DZZlA

Also by David J Cooper

Penny Lane, Paranormal Investigator
The Witch Board
The House of Dolls
The House of Dolls
The Devil's Coins
The Mirror
The Key
The Reveal

Standalone
The Devil Knows
Foul Play
The Devil Knows
The Party's Over
Penny Lane, Paranormal Investigator. Books 1 - 3

Watch for more at davidjcooperauthorblog.wordpress.com.

About the Author

David J Cooper is a British author. He was born in Darlaston, West Midlands, to a working class family. After leaving school he had jobs ranging from engineering to teaching. He got involved in local politics and became a local councillor in 1980.

His novels incorporate elements of the paranormal, horror, suspense, and mystery.

He is featured in the Best Poems and Poets of 2012 with his first and only poem God's Garden.

He currently lives in a small town in Mexico with his three dogs, Chula, Sooty, and Benji.

Read more at davidjcooperauthorblog.wordpress.com.

Printed in Great Britain
by Amazon